I0111919

D

DEDICATION

This book is dedicated to every man and woman across every branch of the military who chose to wear the uniform. On behalf of Pa-Pro-Vi Publishing Company LLC, we thank YOU for YOUR service!

Unknown Battlefields

Pa-Pro-Vi Publishing
presents...

Unknown Battlefields

The Footsteps of a Soldier
A Collection of Stories

~Curtis Abrams~ Mary L. Beal~
~Marvis Cox ~Brandon Dorrington~
~Kevin Eastman~ David Mills~
~Dommartini Salien Sr.~
~Barbara Scandrick-Smith~
~Takia Chase-Smith~

Visionary Author & Publisher
LaQuita Parks

Unknown Battlefields, The Footsteps of a Soldier
A Collection of Stories

Published by Pa-Pro-Vi Publishing
www.paprovipublishing.com

ISBN: 978-1-959667-03-2

Printed in the United States of America

C

CONTENTS

1

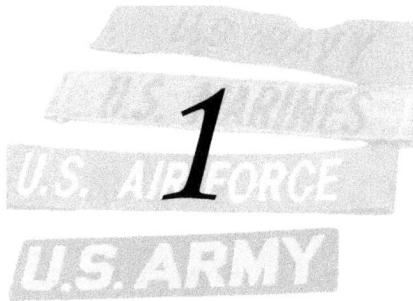

INTRODUCTION

"All that you do, do it with your might, things by half are never done right!" There are a lot of good men and women that I personally know who live by this principal. Although I have never served in the military, half doing anything has always been unacceptable for me.

On August 17, 1955, Dwight D. Eisenhower, the 34th President of the United States, issued Executive Order 10631-Code of Conduct for Members of the Armed Forces of the United States. This code specifies that "All members of the Armed Forces of the United States are required to measure up to the standards that are embodied in the Code of Conduct while in battle or in captivity."

Code of Conduct (https://www.ausa.org/code-conduct)
I am an American fighting in the forces that guard my
country and our way of life,
I am prepared to give my life in their defense.

I will never surrender of my own free will. If in
command, I will never surrender the
members of my command while they still have the
means to resist.

If I am captured, I will continue to resist by all means
available. I will make every
effort to escape and aid others to escape. I will accept
neither parole nor special
favors from the enemy.

If I become a prisoner of war, I will keep faith with my
fellow prisoners. I will give no
information nor take part in any action which might
be harmful to my comrades.
If I am senior, I will take command. If not, I will obey
the lawful orders of those
appointed over me and will back them up in every
way.

Should I become a prisoner of war, I am required to
give name, rank,
service number, and date of birth. I will evade
answering further questions to the utmost of
my ability. I will make no oral or written statements

disloyal to my country and its allies.

I will never forget that I am an American fighting for
freedom, responsible for my actions,
and dedicated to the principles which made my
country free.
I will trust in my God and in the United States of
America.

 The Code of Conduct lets me know that you must be
strong enough for battle because after all... "only the
strong survive!" In 1968, the year before I was born,
Jerry Butler wrote a song called "Only The Strong
Survive." Even though the song is about a man who
gets advice from his mother after a love affair gone
wrong, I connected with the chorus part of the song...
Only the strong survive, Only the strong survive, You
gotta be strong, You better hold on...This rings true
for every aspect of my life and the lives of those who
go into battle because again..." only the strong
survive."

There are a number of reasons one would choose to go
into battle. The word battle, according to Webster's
Dictionary, is defined as, a hostile encounter or
engagement between opposing military forces or
participation in such hostile encounters or
engagements.

Individuals choosing to join the military, do so with
the understanding that they are going to be trained for
"battle." Some join to find a purpose or learn a skill

while others might join as a sense of patriotic duty or a desire to serve their country. Regardless the reason, because of their choice, we are able to enjoy the freedoms we hold so dearly. The collection of stories contained within these pages are the true accounts of the Unknown Battlefields these individuals faced during their service to our country. Whether they saw battle in Vietnam, Desert Storm, Iraq or was a military spouse or rendered dedicated service to the Department of Defense, these are their stories.

LaQuita Parks

Owner/Publisher: Pa-Pro-Vi

2

UNFORGETTABLE- A VETERAN'S WIFE STORY
Barbara Scandrick-Smith

My husband and I were high school sweethearts and so in love that we decided on an early marriage. We got engaged on my 18th birthday. We were married at Travelers Rest Baptist Church on January 10, 1969. My goal had been to become an attorney and wait until we were 25 years old before getting married.

I was going to Georgia State College (now Georgia State University) in Atlanta, Georgia, while my husband worked to supply our needs. He was registered and decided to enlist in the U.S. Army. He was assigned to Fort Knox, Kentucky, for Basic Training in January 1970 after being on delayed entry since October 1969. The delay was to move me back to my mother's home.

The first unknown battleground I can recall was in January 1970. My husband left for duty as a young soldier. It was freezing in Fort Knox. Having to train in the snow, he became ill with pneumonia. I remember receiving a call from the American Red Cross informing me that my husband was hospitalized and in fair condition.

I boarded my first flight from Atlanta to Louisville, Kentucky. I then rode a bus to Fort Knox, where I took my first ride in a taxi to the hospital on Post. These were all "unknown battlegrounds." It was a frightening experience. When I finally arrived at the hospital, my husband had IV needles in both arms, looking pale, very ill, and not eating.

I encouraged him to eat and feed him myself. I stayed at the hospital as long as I was allowed. I then called a taxi for a ride to the Post Guest House around 10:00 p.m. The driver of the cab put me out at the wrong building. Trembling, I walked a few blocks, carrying my small luggage and clutching my purse, in the dark, cold night. When my husband felt better, I returned home to Atlanta.

My husband's next assignment was Fort Rucker, Alabama, where he received advanced individual training as a helicopter mechanic. Before my husband graduated from training, he received orders to report to the Vietnam War after being a soldier for

approximately four months.

One weekend in May, I boarded an airplane for my third flight to Dothan, Alabama. I took a taxi for the long ride to Fort Rucker. My husband was waiting anxiously when I arrived. We had a wonderful time. He showed me around the Post and, of course, we went shopping. While visiting, my husband asked me if I would consider having his baby since he had orders for Vietnam. He said, "If I get killed in Vietnam, at least you will have a part of me," Being so in love, I consented to his request. That weekend, I became pregnant.

My husband came home for a thirty-day leave before reporting to Vietnam. We visited lots of people and spent as much time as we could together. It was painful, my husband leaving me for the unknown and the thought of maneuvering through a pregnancy alone for the next six months. With us both in tears, we said our goodbyes, and he left for Vietnam In August 1970.

Our son was born the following year, on February 19, 1971. He looked exactly like my husband, so I named him the exact same name, Larry Gregory Hunter, Jr. My husband was overjoyed. I could not travel to Hawaii to meet my husband for R&R after his six months absence because I had recently given birth to our son, so we would not see each other for a year.

While in Vietnam, God blessed my husband to be assigned to a position where he could call me often via radio. It was annoying to say "over" after each sentence, but I could, at least, hear his voice and know he was okay. There were times when he would be in the field for weeks, and I had to rely on the Red Cross for status when I did not hear from him. My husband and I wrote to each other every day during the year we were apart. I sent him cassette tapes of our son crying and him cooing in later months. My husband had purchased a Polaroid Instant Camera, so I could send him pictures almost every day. My job was caring for our son and waiting for the mailman each day.

I will never forget the joy I felt when my husband returned from Vietnam on August 21, 1971. His flight landed in Fort Lewis, Washington. He said he kissed the ground and ran to find a telephone to notify me of the good news. He headed home on a flight from Washington but was bumped off the flight.

The military did not greet the soldiers properly. They did not fly them home first class, nor did they arrange for spouses to meet them in Washington. My husband was anxious to get home, so he boarded a Greyhound bus for the long ride to Atlanta. When he called to notify me that he was in the United States and on his way home, I showered and put on my best outfit to receive him.

I still remember the anxiety of waiting to see my husband again and introducing him to his son, looking into his eyes, and our long delicious kiss. It was so wonderful being back in my husband's arms again. Our beautiful life together restarted! The next day after my husband's return from Vietnam, we went out, and my husband purchased me a brand-new black sports car.

After 30 days in Atlanta, our little family packed the car and headed to Fort Hood, Texas, my first real battleground as a military wife. It was a very long trip. We stayed overnight at a Hotel in Shreveport, Louisiana, and continued our journey the following morning. Nothing was a complaint for us. We were back together, where we belonged.

We finally arrived in Texas, where we rented our first home away from home. It was a small duplex in Killeen, Texas, a military town outside the Fort Hood gate where my husband was stationed. I was homesick and bored while my husband worked, but our love allowed me to manage. I had my car, but it was a small town with nowhere to go.

I had always been sheltered and protected. Being away from home and my family was definitely an unknown battleground I knew I had to battle. I called my mama almost every day and indulged in lots of prayers. I mastered the military's plan as the Army managed my husband's life with their orders.

My husband was promoted to Sergeant in Vietnam because he was an excellent soldier with great ratings. He earned a lot of opportunities and quite a bit of freedom. My husband drove me home nine times during the three years we lived in Texas. My mother, grandmother, sister, and niece visited us for a week in

1972, the first year I was away from home.

We purchased a beautiful new mobile home in 1973, and my mother came to Texas for her second visit. Letters, pictures, and phone calls from family, friends, and mostly from my mama helped to heal my battleground wounds. In May 1974, my husband received orders for Hawaii shortly after I had become pregnant again. Sadly, we decided to sell our mobile home with no profit. We were uncomfortable renting it out in our absence, and we knew being apart was not an option.

We traveled to Atlanta for 30 days to visit our families, then on the road again to deliver our automobile to Oakland, California, to be shipped to Hawaii. It was 2,500 miles journey to San Francisco. The speed limit had been reduced to 55 mph, so the drive was challenging, although we cheated and drove much faster than we should have. Luckily, we were not stopped by the policeman. The drive took all of seven days.

Due to my pregnancy, the doctor gave strict orders for travel if I was to ride as opposed to fly. We drove, talked, and sang. We were instructed to take breaks every two hours. We had each other and our 3 years old baby boy. We were so happy. We did lots of sightseeing as we drove through Alabama, Mississippi, Louisiana, Texas, Mexico, and Arizona. We finally arrived in San Francisco. California. I felt like I never wanted to take another automobile trip. We toured the city for three days before taking our automobile across the bridge to Oakland to be shipped. We then boarded the Southwestern Orient Airlines for the five-hour flight across the Pacific Ocean to Honolulu, Hawaii, where we would live at Schofield Barracks for the next three years. After arriving, our tour was changed to 39 months, six months longer.

It was a bit tough adjusting at first. The time zone was five hours behind the central time in Texas we had grown accustomed to while living there. We had to live in a temporary hotel (living in one room and out of luggage) for thirty days. To make matters worse, our automobile was not expected to arrive for thirty days. We rented a home in Wahiawa, Hawaii, a Hawaiian community, for six months.

After three months and being almost eight months pregnant, my husband was working overnight duty when my bags ruptured, and I went into premature labor. After three days of harsh labor, another son was born, weighing 4 pounds 3 ounces. My husband had the privilege to name him Andre' Lamont Hunter. That was a battlefield. My husband took 30 days off work to care for me and our oldest. He drove to Honolulu each day to check on our newborn baby. After that scare, my husband applied for quarters on Post at Schofield Barracks.

It was 3 months before we were approved and able to move. We were blessed to be assigned housing a few feet from my husband's job. He came home regularly to check on us. It was different, living on an island that took approximately ninety minutes to drive around the entire Oahu Island. We would drive to Honolulu every evening, go to the mall, Waikiki Beach, and International Market Place, and mingle with visiting tourists. The stores were open all night.

This was an unknown battleground, very different from our way of life. We had no heaters or air conditioners. The weather was very mild. Shorts and thongs (shoes) were our daily attire, even during winter. Our primary activity every week was our trips to the beach. We also went on the Pearl Harbor Cruise in Honolulu three times.

That was one of the major attractions for our guests. We were not allowed to transport our furniture to Hawaii, so we had to accept assigned standard furniture. We were able to choose our living room set from three basic colors. We eventually purchased our furniture, and the government shipped it to our next unknown battleground duty station.

Being In the military became expensive, although quarters allowance was automatically taken from soldier's checks, and there was no charge for any utilities. Each new duty station had different measurements. We constantly had to purchase curtains and other items to accommodate our taste in each dwelling away from home. We had so many colors and sizes of curtains, bathroom, and kitchen items that we could have opened a store. At each change of station, we had to locate a suitable church and licensed beautician to keep my hair healthy. My husband would shampoo, straighten, and roll my hair until we could accomplish that task. He was a "Jack of all trades."

In 1977, it was time to return to the Mainland. It was a great feeling to be back on familiar soil. I left Hawaii and stayed in Atlanta for 3 months due to circumstances I attended to. Fortunately, my husband received new orders through God's favor and was stationed at Fort Benning, Georgia (Columbus), our home state. We were only two hours from Atlanta. Our bank account suffered because we came home every weekend to visit family and for entertainment. At Fort Benning, we purchased new furniture, which I still have today.

I love antiques! We came home on Fridays and stayed until Sunday night, leaving in time for my husband to report to duty on Monday morning. It was a blessing being home often and on holidays. We met new friends, and some joined us in visiting on weekends, excited about Atlanta, the big city in the South that they had heard so much about but had never visited. Each tour was an adjustment. It was an unknown battleground, being in a new, unfamiliar home, spending nights alone and unable to sleep when my husband was on duty.

He would sometimes leave the boys and me for 30 days of training. In July 1979, our weekly trips to Atlanta and our family fellowship halted when my husband received orders for Hanau, Germany. We, again, had to up route and prepare to travel to another unknown battleground. My husband and I had to separate again for the first time in almost nine years.

He cleared Fort Benning after going through the inspection to make sure our quarters passed. We sold one of our cars since we were not shipping them to Europe. We had purchased a new car, and unfortunately, we had mechanical problems the day we were to leave for Atlanta. This was the first time the military did not allow us concurrent travel. My husband moved my sons and me to Atlanta for 2 months until he could report to Europe and secure our temporary housing.

In September 1979, my two sons and I boarded a flight for our destination to Germany. I was sad/happy as we boarded the jet for our flight out of Hartsfield Jackson Atlanta Airport. I was sad to leave my mama but happy that we would be joining my husband, who we had not seen in over a month. We flew to Philadelphia and then to Fort Dix, New Jersey. This was the first time we had flown on a military flight, and it was not smooth at all.

For the first time, we flew out of our native country to the unknown. We arrived in Frankfurt, Germany, and were greeted by my husband. I will never forget the "jet lag. As a result of the time zone change of Europe being six hours ahead of Eastern time in Atlanta and disturbing my sleep pattern, I felt as if I had been drugged and would never be able to get sufficient sleep. It was terrible.

The children had to report to school. I would wake up, take them to the bus stop, rush back home, and set the alarm clock to wake up in time to go back to the bus stop to pick them up. It took about three weeks for me to get enough sleep to function. I never in my life experienced anything as harsh as that. We also had temporary housing, which was a huge place with a long hallway.

It was odd looking from the outside and had eight bedrooms. That in itself was scary, but I was too sleepy at first to be affected. By Christmas, we had moved into our regular quarters, where we would be assigned to live for the next three years. It was very different. It was called stairwell living. We were not accustomed to ever living in apartment-type housing with assigned parking spaces and people across the stairwell and upstairs over us.

We had no washer and dryer connections and had to have the old standard military furniture again. We had assigned wash days with the other eight families in the building. This was the worse! My sons were in school, so despite my husband not wanting me to work, I had gotten my International Driver's License and a Volkswagen as our second automobile. I learned my way around and knew enough German language to do transactions and greetings.

It was a terrible battleground. To cope with my dissatisfaction, I secured a job on Post, a couple of blocks from our quarters, working as Secretary/Procurement Clerk for the Colonel and Sergeant Major in the Hanau Area Club System Headquarters NCO and Officers Clubs. It was a fun job with benefits. I got all the publicity, and we were able to attend the shows when singers came to Europe to perform and do other activities at no cost.

I really was missing my mama. This was the furthest I had ever been away from her. I could manage as long as I had a telephone and an automobile. Telephone fees were so high by the minute that we could not afford to call often, but mama always came through and would call us at unexpected times and more often than we expected.

Most families did have either and could not master the difficult exam and determination to receive the International Driver's License. The other problem was rations on gasoline, coffee, liquor, and tea. We did not drink liquor, and my husband seldom drank coffee. We could do without tea, so we traded our tea, liquor, and coffee rations for gasoline rations for both of our automobiles. We learned our way all over Germany, visiting other cities. The other plus is that my brother was stationed in Europe while we were there.

They did not have a vehicle, but my husband would pick them up most Saturday mornings, and they would stay at our home until Sunday night before he would take them back to Wiesbaden, Germany, where we loved to shop at their area Post Exchange. I even got my first and only train ride in Europe. We left Frankfurt and rode the train to Wiesbaden. It was frightening going through and traveling at a very high speed.

The constant snowstorms and blizzards became a big part of our German life experience. My mama visited us for three weeks in 1980, so we traveled a lot. We visited Paris, Holland, four German cities, and the many attractions in Europe. It was still a welcomed day when it came time to return to the United States.

We returned to the United States with orders to return to our first military home away from home, Fort Hood, Texas. Before leaving, I lived in Atlanta for seven months, securing a job at Cox Cable Communications. We went to Texas where we rented a home. There was more to decorate, so we shopped every day. I feared all the tornadoes in Texas, and sometimes I would be caught home alone with our two sons. The other thing was the heat. We had never experienced such high temperatures, over 100 degrees. My mama came to visit and would stand under the tree until I started the car and had the air going. I never liked Texas but enjoyed that we could visit Dallas, San Antonio, and Austin every week since it was only an hour from our home.

My battlegrounds were easier after the tour in Germany. After living there, I feel I could have lived anywhere in the States. I was still uncomfortable with my husband being gone at night or away for days of training. The challenge came when my husband became more and more overprotective of me, not controlling, as he had been since we were 16 years old, when he would drive miles from his house to our home to pick me up for school and bring me back home each afternoon. He even joined my church to be in my presence all day on Sundays.

Since our boys were in school, my husband was at work, and I had my own automobile, it was time to secure a job and utilize my skills. I mastered the state test and was hired. My husband could not understand why I wanted to work when he could care for us. He always gave me his check, and I managed everything, even the spending. He was always sending and bringing flowers to my office and making pop-up visits. For the first time, I sensed his insecurity. I worked six months with the battleground of a jealous, insecure, stressed husband because I had no intention of quitting my job.

In deep thought, I finally decided to make my life's most difficult unknown battleground decision. Not knowing if it would complicate things, I knew I had to make an ultimate decision. I knew how much my husband loved our boys and me and how much we loved him, but I had faith in my corner. Not going into detail in this setting, I decided to divorce my husband.

All hell broke loose when I shared my decision with him. My husband did not receive my decision to divorce him well. I made a getaway plan, maneuvered through it, and was successful.

I will never forget the unknown battlegrounds encountered as a military wife. I experienced challenges compared to none other when I packed up at 21 years old and left home for the first time, not to return permanently for many years. I encountered battleground after battleground and move after move. I am not saying it was not enjoyable, because it was, but it was unknown, which was sometimes a little uncomfortable, like walking blindfolded.

The Army was a battlefield for our two sons, as well. They were forced to change schools and leave their friends when their daddy received unexpected orders; it was time to move on to the next battleground. Our sons never complained. We never left our boys in the care of anyone else. They knew we would be there to protect and support them. That is one reason I never desired to work before they were both school-age and even beyond.

The military offers excellent travel exposure opportunities, seeing how other ethnicities survive and their way of life, meeting new life-long friends, and growing in many ways. It is an educational opportunity with so much exposure. The military is a good, comfortable life, but in all honesty, it focuses more on the soldier than the spouse and children. In my experience, I gave up my education and other opportunities, sometimes being left alone to give birth and raise the children. When my husband was commanded to answer the call of duty, sometimes given an assignment to be in war operation, away at times for 30 days of training and overnight duty or test flights. It was a great experience with unknown battlegrounds, as a wife, not knowing what to expect, even the possibility of being suddenly ordered to war or the fear that he would be a casualty.

In Vietnam, he received Air Medals and a Bronze Star for being a Hero, exposing himself to enemy fire to assist one soldier after pulling another soldier from a helicopter that had been shot down. He administered first aid when the soldiers were being transported to a medical facility, but they both died. I did not know my husband was in such danger until he returned home with medals. My husband was a wonderful, supportive husband and father, but his every breath was for me.

Many would have loved that, but I have always been secure, which sets me aside from most women. I began feeling smothered, although I had my own vehicle, his money, and my freedom. My husband did everything for me, including cooking. He bought a sewing machine because I said I would learn to sew, but he learned and mastered it very well. I never sewed a stitch, never baked a cookie, cake, or bread. He could do anything he decided and did it all well. I was just the Queen of the House.

I divorced my high school sweetheart and love and began an unknown journey of my own. Even after many years, my ex-husband always told me that we should never have been divorced. He said that he was jealous and I was spoiled. I believe it was a marriage made in heaven, and we were meant to meet in the school band room and begin a long relationship. It can be detrimental when we do not follow God's order in our lives.

After moving back to Atlanta, I secured employment and retired from the State of Georgia with a tenure of almost 20 years, retiring 13 years ago in 2009. I remarried for 20 years before initiating the divorce. My ex-husband has been deceased for 9 months, but I will never forget him and the experiences we shared. He remarried 3 times, but we both always knew that God created us for each other.

My ex-husband helped to create many chapters in my life that made me the strong mature woman I am today. Had I not given up on him, there is no telling where life would have taken us. We experienced and grew together. We both vowed to love each other to the end, and we did. I will never forget our last long conversation, just two months before his transition. He shared his concern about his illness and the doctor's treatment plan. I assured him I would pray and reminded him of God's healing power.

I thank God for the Unknown Battlegrounds and the many blessings resulting from this faithful journey in my life.

Barbara Scandrick-Smith is always loving, kind, giving and compassionate. She meets no strangers, has a magnetic personality, knowledgeable and has a knack for getting along with others. Barbara's greatest qualities are her keen mind, leadership skills and her ability to communicate and compile correspondence. She always brightens the corner where she is and leaves a lasting impression. Barbara enjoys writing, decorating, planning functions, fashion, family, and antiques. She is a collector of eggs, elephants, books, and over 600 record albums. Barbara now resides in Clayton County, Georgia where she has lived the past 40 years since returning to Georgia after a lengthy military wife journey.

3

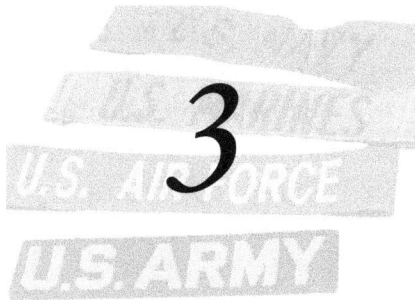

COMRADE
Brandon Dorrington

It was my first semester during my senior year in high school when I enrolled in the U.S Army Delayed Entry Program. I would contemplate graduation, basic training, and a productive military career every day after school. The chain of events that ultimately led to my service separation was very unusual but what remained constant was my commitment to service.

First, I vividly remember the day when my recruiter dropped me off at the airport to depart for basic training in Ft. Benning, GA. My heart was pounding, my blood pressure rose extremely high, and I felt like dying. However, I displayed leadership within the team of fellow recruits to ensure we all arrived at training successfully.

The first day at my initial duty station was the 101st Airborne Division NCO Academy. After recently completing basic and advanced individual training and becoming a full-fledged soldier, I was ready to start kicking ass and taking names until I was ordered to continue training.

I spent the next twelve months at the primary leadership development course until I finally got a date to attend my first of many selection programs. Loudly, lock and load echoed as we began our first combat patrol in Theater. The moment finally arrived to use everything I learned during training on a real-world mission.

The infantryman's creed, battle drills, and range expectations had been previously internalized and embodied in me. Now it is the last ninety days of my extended enlistment, and I'm no longer the best student in Air Assault, Airborne, and Ranger school or any other program I once attended.

The current perception of reality is that I'm a quitter, coward, and fugitive. However, I'm more motivated, dedicated, and fired up than ever to support, fight, and lead my brothers in arms to victory but not in the light, only from the shadows. Secrecy is my only way of life, even though my character was tarnished. After all, I'm a true comrade.

Brandon Dorrington is an Advisory Council Member at Bastion Community of Resilience. He has a Master of Arts in Criminal Justice and currently resides in New Orleans, LA., Brandon's skills include documentaries and research writing (Veterans Journey Home and Positivist vs Classical School of Thought.

Brandon enjoys fasting, mountain climbing and rifling.

4

THE AUTHORITY OF A RAW PARADISE
Curtis Abrams

"The power in the energy lies beneath the bliss of the innate as which views the lack. "Curtis Abrams Jr.

Have you ever really glanced at the beauty that nature created? I mean, take a look at the yellow daffodils and the hibiscus in the heavily evergreen area. My favorite one is purple hydrangea so I pick it up; I was told this particular flower requires pure water hydration and symbolizes a need for total forgiveness. If you're making amends with a friend or loved one take this one.

Waegwan, South Korea, was my duty station from 1995 to 1996. I quit smoking when I was there on New Year's Day in 1996. My assignment was to work in the motor pool and to assist the Motor Sergeant with having the wheel vehicles for our company in the 6th Ordinance Battalion located in Camp Carroll, South Korea, by Taegu. We had the opportunity to leave the military post and tour the town. I always loved to go to the natural wilderness part of the bushes and high trees that surrounds the Waegwan area.

I'm so addicted every time I enter the beauty and the wilderness of the field and the sunshine that radiates the garden. I love the smell of flowers to enhance my senses and alleviate my hunger, so I won't smoke again. Imagine the beautiful texture and the scent of the hydrangea flower throughout the backyard and the green pasture throughout the South Korean spring beech forest. For some reason, I heard a loud noise and nature turns into a battlefield.
As I look around the nature of the wilderness.

A colossal bomb explodes. I run back to the tent. The day quickly turns into night. I grab my M-16 rifle. A herd of quick, young Korean soldiers invades my territory with heavy, loud gunfire. Another bomb goes off and destroys a nearby tent. The sound is deafening my ears.

An enemy comes in my direction, and I answer with fire from my M-16. He falls quickly. As I look upward, the entire flower patch is covered with blood and bodies everywhere, screaming and crying. I'm petrified and paranoid; then I touch the flower, I feel a hard hand shaking my back, and then....

I felt a hard kick!

"Wake up, you're going to be late," was my Korean military roommate friend. He is called KATUSA (Korean Augmented Troops of the United States Army. And I am 5 minutes late for formation. This is the third time this week that I'm about to be late." Hold it hold it!! You two wait right there. The First Sergeant calls me out before I even make another move; I freeze, and he says stand over there and wait.

Everybody else was standing in formation, getting ready for the today. The First Sergeant came upon me and put on a pleasant smile, and ask with his grin and teeth, "What the hell are you doing, Specialist, smelling the daisies? Why are you sleeping?" As I was grinning a little bit and was about to answer, I was saved by our company commander, who needed to talk to the First Sergeant about a meeting they had to go to immediately. So, he glanced at me and told me to drop and do 50 and return to formation. It was a sigh of relief. I apologize to my Korean roommate, and we stand in line.

I was one of the few military soldiers of color on that peninsula. As I finished working that day in the motor pool on base, I left the post and walked throughout the town. Everyone seemed joyful, pleasant, and friendly as I glanced at the people. As I think about

the military soldiers on the post, everybody keeps to themselves. No one is conforming to one another. But when I leave the post, I'll look at a different side of culture in the eastern hemisphere. Everyone is laughing and running around. There is playing of all ages, and quite frankly, everyone seems free despite the working conditions in their moderate environment. No one seems upset, shocked, stressed, mad, or violent. This is remarkably interesting to me.

Before I came to Korea, I was in Colorado Springs, another area where some of the populations were Native American or white. Not many minorities were in that state as well. I looked at how that culture is displayed. I am a 19-year-old farm boy from Tuscaloosa, AL, who comes from my own individualistic identity as the outlier or the outsider of the bunch. There is fear as I go through these military bases because I have no one to support me. In Colorado, everybody is on their own. No one cares about anyone but themselves. Being on your own, you must be very mindful of your surroundings.

I got into fights, had to defend myself verbally, and reminded people that I was representing the U.S. Army. I could not be involved in anything detrimental to my character. So I made many friends in Colorado, however, something significant in South Korea changed my way of being part of society forever.

We have all been prepared and nurtured differently. In the military world, you are disciplined and motivated to defend your country at the price of freedom and independence for everyone worldwide. When you are on your own, having discipline in your own right is envisioning your contentment in how society conforms. It's up to you to take the challenge for total freedom of independence.

This is not to imply that when I was on the military base in Korea, the experience of being a soldier was horrible. Being overseas and representing my country halfway around the world in such an honor was my right. The behavior, along with the army conduct and the environment, was more stringent. Rightfully so, you are in a hostile climate overseas, so you must be alert every time. If something happens, you must also be mindful of an alert for any military operation.

As my Korean KATUSA walked along, he showed me many cultures and customs that the U.S. doesn't care to relate to. First, we ate at a local Korean restaurant. The food was delicious, kimchi (a rotten spicy cabbage that is healthy in the Korean culture) along with ramen noodles, "yaki mandu" Korean dumplings with a hot bowl of soy sauce and washing it down with SoJu made from rice and barley. I felt a buzz when I drank the colorless beverage with alcohol.

Then, he showed me that when people sit down and eat a meal on a tray, everybody comes around and shares the tray so everyone can eat at once. I said to myself I had never seen that in my culture. Will you eat by yourself? You don't want anyone to hover around your plate? I've also noticed they play sports altogether, leaving no one behind.

In contrast, everything in the U.S. culture is isolation, individual motivation, and preparation, somewhat similar to an athlete preparing alone to compete at an event. Even teamwork perpetually preached. Sometimes they'll cut you from the team if you're not good enough, but there, everyone works together. Everyone travels together in that country; they wander into the woods and look at nature. They have taverns and cave entrances for discovery, they go to museums together as one, and they make up tents at night outside and sleep altogether.

When they wake up in the morning and dress up, they check each other out before leaving. Whereas when you are by yourself, you have to dress by yourself or take a shower and do hygiene. Every Korean face I've seen seems to be the happiest they've ever been, even though they don't have any money or transportation. They walk everywhere and are joyous about their destination. I thought, "this is incredible" I've never seen anything like this in my 22 years of life.

I went along with them and being the only U.S. lone wolf in the bunch; they welcomed me with open arms. For the first time in my young adult life, I felt I belonged to something; I could not even feel that way in high school because I was different from anyone else. They took me for who I was, asked me questions, and wanted me to be their friend, a "U.S. guy." The feeling was beautiful. For once, I didn't feel ostracized. There was a tear in my eye, and they told me not to cry but to be happy.

I felt pretty isolated in Colorado Springs because I wasn't with my immediate family but doing things on my own was my plan. There was a level of fear and uncertainty. Here I felt like I was essential or a hero. It's a genuine feeling I have to this day, just like the hydrangea.

It was just the overall beauty of being in that area of the world, from the warm summer days to the rainy monsoon seasons, to the cold wind covering the mountains in the wintertime. That place has covered me like a blanket to keep me warm and secure from any insecurities I may have within myself.

I didn't want to leave South Korea in 1996, but I was re-assigned to the 3rd Battalion, 15th Infantry in Fort Stewart, GA. The Korean community gave me a going-away party. It was a lot of Koreans there. We did a karaoke contest and a cake, and everybody sang in the Hangul language. Then, they hugged me in unison and told me, good luck with your next adventure. I have to say, I wanted to leave Colorado simply because I felt isolated. I had no sense of warmth and conformity or acquaintances to which I could relate... only a few, but no one really.

I didn't want to leave Korea, ever. I will never forget what the captain of my Battalion told me before I left South Korea in 1996. He told me I was strong-minded and reminded me about gratifying my choices. What you see beyond your view can be completely different based on your intended purpose, and no path is apparent until you support your choice. You must never lose focus, ever! He gave me a salute, and I followed with a return salute.

The Korean culture is primarily loyal and sincere when you meet; they're kind and show tremendous respect to the family and elderly. On the other hand, the Asian culture ascertains a form of collectivism. Individuals are attached to their group identity, and the sense of being self-sufficient is not relevant or essential to wildlife.

Curiosity can be a significant benefactor in wanting to know how different culture is when someone foreign enters a territory. There is something fresh, but curious about the experience. Whether accepting the differences in social interaction or being isolated and feeling lonely, there is something to be said about being embedded in such a group.

Maybe foreigners are taken more seriously than their local counterparts, then maybe not. Regardless, you must be very aware and cautious of the surroundings of people you don't know. If I'm on another planet and if people I encounter don't look the same as I do, but we have the same feeling and interactions, then it shouldn't be a problem to start engaging from the beginning with someone to understand their internal values.

I can still smell the tulips, hibiscus, and hydrangea, as well as the daffodils throughout the whole area. The smell never goes away. The hospitality of everyone with Korean blood was nothing short of unforgettable, with a carefree spirit. I have to say, if there were a Utopian slice of heaven, it was in Waegwan, Taegu area in the South Korean peninsula.

I traveled back to Tuscaloosa, Alabama, to visit my family and friends for a thirty-day paid leave, before heading to Fort Stewart, Ga. My perspective on people as a culture has changed drastically for the betterment of good. I have become more aware of what to expect when approaching anyone who wants to belong and be accepted. I have great love and generosity without an ounce of hate in my body and salvation in my soul. We, indeed, as humans, need to feed into our insight. We should understand what we are sacrificing our minds and bodies for.

I sometimes go out to walk through the patch of wilderness by the area of Lake Tuscaloosa. I looked at the fish swimming across the creek as clearly as I could. I witnessed their path to freedom, and as I walked gingerly through the island leaves in the dry brown twigs going uphill, I spotted a deer looking directly at and strolling towards me. Neither of us moves. Just there looking at each other as if time stood still. He looks up and runs away.

As I'm in the forest all by myself, as if already in South Korea, this great power of synergy comes towards me from the rays of the sunshine. Indicating that even though I am in a world of discipline and uniformity, I can always have a sense of total internal liberation within myself. Hence, I must not have intrusive thoughts about how I react to any form of negativity in people and situations.

I will respect my superiors and my chain of command if they need me to complete a task. I will decide to use my natural abilities and instinct to meet any challenges and any job that is adequate for me. I still live with that mantra today, thanks to my acquiescence to the warmth of nature, the beautiful flowers I've discovered in South Korea, and the overall experience I felt internally from a collectivist standpoint.

I don't feel isolated anymore based on overcoming my fear of uncertainty. I know I'm going to die only once. If I am going to become a representative of my self-identity, then I will assess any challenges that come my way at my discretion. However, I will not let any obstacles I face exacerbate my focus on reality, and I will formulate my intuition as much as possible by serving my country and the people who live in it.

As I prepared for my next duty station in Fort Stewart, GA. I make a trip to the University of Alabama Arboretum area. I looked at the many gardens and the flowers that encompassed the beauty of such an environment. As I walked up the hill of the forest-like site, I noticed something very familiar. A tear runs from my eye, and I see the same hydrangea blooming flower I witnessed in South Korea a few months ago. I feel vindicated that my fears of being open and isolated have now gone away by looking at this beautiful flower, a symbol of my total deliverance. I was about to touch this excellent flower at the Arboretum, and someone behind me tapped my shoulder, said hi, and told me that the flower was beautiful. The woman looks young and Asian, possibly of Korean descent. So I told her in Hangul do you like this flower. And she responded with a nod.

Ask yourself, which world of an indicative way of life you would prefer? The discipline of preserving and supporting the fight for your freedom to honor your country or the ability to enjoy being authentic by basking in that raw, spiritual freedom of being decisive based on your cultural view of society. You have the power source to choose from. You can choose to live carefree internally until the definitive end.

Curtis Abrams has studied and worked in Behavior and Social Psychology for over 15 years. A native of Tuscaloosa, Alabama, and currently resides in Florida. Curtis has been an introvert and a loner most of his life. He is now a licensed professional home and commercial insurance claims adjuster and inspector for the State of Florida. Curtis is a licensed tutor who mentors and volunteers at public and private schools in Florida. A University of Alabama graduate with a Communications degree.

Curtis also served in the U.S. Army for 10 years and has traveled throughout the world to learn about different social cultures. In addition, he's an avid writer of short stories, periodically blogs online, and create online content for personal development and social awareness.

Curtis is training to become a personal life coach so he can educate and inspire others all over the world to thrive and succeed.
He is a father of a son and a daughter and is currently learning how to play the acoustic guitar and keyboard for his inner peace.

5

MY PTSD STORY
(TAKEN FROM MY "WAR & PTSD PODCAST)
David Mills

My name is Dave Mills. I am 72 years old and a US Navy Veteran. I joined the US Navy in 1968, when I was 19 years old. At that time, the Vietnam War was in full swing.

There are several reasons why I joined the US Navy.

I went to college...for a few semesters...then after 13 years of public school...I lost interest in continuing my education and began looking for something else to do.

One thing that I could do...was join one of the branches of the US military. The Vietnam War was ramping up...and because I was not in college any longer...I was no longer deferred from the military draft. Because of that, it wouldn't be long before Uncle Sam would come calling on me...and then I would be drafted into the US Army.

An alternative to the military was a full-time job.

But, I wasn't really interested in that either...so between school...a full-time job...and the military...I decided to go with the military...and I joined the US Navy.

I signed up at my local recruiter's office...and soon after that I received a letter from the United States Naval Personnel office...telling me to report to Navy boot camp in San Diego, California.

After boot camp, I received orders to report to the USS Maddox, in Long Beach, California. The Maddox was classified as a Destroyer.

As I walked up the ship's gangplank...fresh from boot camp...I was told that this ship had two departments that needed more sailors. The first, was in the boiler department. Those sailors worked in the boiler room of the ship. The second was the propulsion department. Sailors in that department were enginemen, who worked in the ship's diesel – engine room.

There were four of us that were boarding the ship from boot camp that day. As we walked up the gangplank, they gave each of us a number from one to four. Mine was number three. Number one and three were assigned to the Engine room...and two and four were assigned to the Boiler room.

That was a lucky day for me...because the boiler room was hot, steamy, and sweaty...while the engine room was air conditioned.

The first thing my shipmates told me about the Maddox...was that it was the ship that started the war in Vietnam. They told me that on August 2, 1964, several North Vietnamese patrol torpedo boats attacked the USS Maddox. At that time, the Maddox was in international waters...not illegally   the coastline of North Vietnam.

Because of this...the attack on the USS Maddox was considered an unprovoked attack on a foreign ship in international waters.

As a result...President Lyndon B. Johnson, used this situation to increase the number of US ground troops in South Vietnam.

I had been on the Maddox about five months...when we went on a training exercise 100 miles off the shore of California. For the past few months, I'd been seeing a lot in the news about how bad our troops were doing in South Vietnam. It was starting to get to me.

I felt like I wasn't doing my part in fighting the war, by just sitting around on a ship...off the California shore. What was going on in Vietnam sounded a lot more exciting to me.

So, I decided to volunteer to go to South Vietnam and fight in the war.

A few months later, I received orders to report to Ton Sun Nhut Air Base in Saigon, South Vietnam.

Spending a year in South Vietnam...fighting a war, was an interesting and exciting experience. But, the sum total of my experiences during that year in Vietnam...created my PTSD.

My experiences in Vietnam caused my PTSD and negatively changed my life.

Today...50 years later...I am finally able to deal with the abnormal personality traits...the irrational attitudes...the dysfunctional behaviors...and the destructive relationships...that were developed...as a result of my PTSD.

War is Hell?! My guess is that a person can only understand that statement, if they have been in a war situation. For me, my experience in Vietnam in 1969 was pure Hell.

When I got off the plane in the Tan Son Nhut Air base in Saigon, Vietnam, I was anxious and wide-eyed. I had no idea what to expect. As my group departed from the plane, we were told to look out for mortar shells that could be dropped near the base at any time. I had no idea what that would look like, but it scared the bejeebees out of me.

We were all sent to a military Transition House in

Saigon, where I spent a week, before I was transferred to my first duty station.

In October of 1969, I was transferred to the Cat Lo Naval Base near Vung Tau, Vietnam.

The Cat Lo Navy base was a repair dock for Swift Boats. A Swift Boat is like a cabin cruiser that is outfitted with twin diesel engines and lots of machine guns.

These boats patrol the coast of Vietnam and sometime go up the rivers in the Mekong Delta region of South Vietnam.

I was a mechanic on the diesel engines in those boats. However, I was not a good mechanic, so I did most of the grunt work.

When the propellers on one of these boats needed to be replaced, my boss would send me up to the warehouse to get 2 of them. I would grab two propellers, put one on each shoulder and heft them back to the dock. They weighed about 50 pounds each and were about 2' in diameter.

My first encounter with the enemy in Vietnam, happened one evening, just after dark. I was in my barracks when I heard several gun shots that were spread throughout the base.

This was the first time I had heard gun shots on the base, so I asked the guys I was with, what was going on. They said they didn't know, but I was to stay inside the barracks.

A few minutes later, they said they had just found out that a Viet Cong sniper was set up outside the base, shooting randomly into the barracks.

We were locked down for about ½ hour. Then an announcement came, that the sniper had been secured, (whatever that meant), and the base was now secure.

I did not find out what happened to the sniper, or if he caused any damage in the base.

In November of 1969, I was assigned to a new unit called the KSB Unit.

The KSB unit was put together, when an Admiral and a General got together at a party one evening, and the General told the Admiral that he had 50 ski boats, with Johnson outboard motors on them, and 50 caliber machine guns that could be mounted on the bow. The General said that he had no use for them. The boats had never been used, and they were still in their original crates in an army depot.

The Admiral said he could use them...and the KSB Unit was born.

In November of 1969, I was sent back to Saigon from Cat Lo, where I met up with my new KSB Unit. The unit consisted of 5 sailors, who worked with fiberglass, 5 outboard motor mechanics, a Petty Officer 2nd Class, who was our supervisor, and a

Lieutenant that was our commander. We were a new and very independent unit. I had no idea who, or what, department of the Navy, that our unit reported to.

Our new unit was assigned to an LST that would be carrying us and our ski boats to the YRBM 16 on the Chau Doc River, in the Mekong Delta area. That is where we were going to be stationed.

The 50 Kenner Ski Boats were still in their wooden crates on the LST when we got there. Our job was to break them out of their crates and assemble their various parts, including the outboard engines, and get them operational.

That is what we did for the three weeks that it took us to get up the river, to our permanent duty station. Because we were on a deadline to have all 50 boats uncrated, assembled, and operational before we got to the YRBM 16, we were required to work 12-hour days, 7 days a week, for 3 weeks, uncrating and assembling the ski boats.

We were told that when we got the ski boats put together, that we would hand them over to a unit of 50 South Vietnamese soldiers that were also going to be assigned to our unit.

Those soldiers were to use the boats to set up nightly patrols along the Vinh Te Canal, to ambush North Vietnamese Soldiers attempting to enter South Vietnam from Cambodia.

The Navy and I got off on the wrong foot from the very beginning of this assignment. It was going to take us about 3 weeks to get to our permanent duty station on the Bassac River, near the town of Chao Doc.

This did not go over well with the guys in our newly, thrown together unit. From the start, our supervisors – the 2nd class Petty Officer and the Lieutenant – showed little concern for the task we were assigned. Their orders were to get the boats operational, and our orders were to assemble the boats before we reached our destination.

That was OK, until we started having problems assembling boats, that we knew nothing about. When we had a question about assembling a part of the boat, we had to hunt down our supervisors to see if they could help us find the answer to our problem. We would consistently find them, sitting in the cafeteria drinking coffee.

Not only, were they not available, but they did not want anything to do with assembling the boats. They said the assembly was our job and for us to figure it out. This did not make us happy campers from the start. And it got worse from there.

When we got to our permanent duty station, it turned out to be a floating barge, moored in the middle of the Bassac River, next to the village of Chao Doc. The river was about 2 blocks wide and ran from Chau Doc, along the Cambodia border down to the South China

Sea.

Chau Doc was a medium sized town that was about 75 miles from the nearest large city.

We sailed past the YRBM 16...to a floating dock, that was anchored in the middle of the river. That is the place we were going to call home, for the next few months. By then, we had most of the ski boats...put together and running.

We unloaded them from the LST...and tied them to our floating dock, in the middle of the Chau Doc River.

This floating dock...was where the 10 members of our KSB Unit...and the 50 South Vietnamese Army soldiers were going to bunk. We were all going to be living together on that floating dock.

All we did...was sleep there. We had our meals on the YRBM 16, which was also anchored in the middle of the Chau Doc River...about six blocks upriver, from our dock.

The floating barge we were living on was about 75 feet long and 30 feet wide. All it had on it were the bunks for 50 South Vietnamese soldiers, and the 12 of us in the KSB unit. Our bunks were surrounded by thin metal walls and covered with a canvas top.

We ate our meals, cleaned up, and relaxed on the YRBM 16, which acted as a floating hotel for us. It was also moored in the middle of the river about six blocks from our floating barge.

The reason our KSB unit was formed, was so the South Vietnamese soldiers could patrol the Vinh Te canal and stop the North Vietnamese soldiers from coming into South Vietnam from Cambodia.

The North Vietnamese soldiers were leaving North Vietnam, going into Laos, down to Cambodia, and across the Vinh Te canal into South Vietnam.

The purpose of the nightly patrols that the South Vietnamese soldiers were setting up, was to capture or kill the North Vietnamese Army soldiers, as they tried to cross over to South Vietnam.

The canal was about 50 miles long, so the South Vietnamese soldiers were to set up ambushes, about every mile along the canal. The width of the canal ranged from 20 feet to 100 ft wide.

My job in the KSB Unit was to repair the outboard motors on the boats. I was one of the five outboard motor mechanics assigned to the Unit. The other five sailors were fiberglass repair people.

We rode our boats from the floating dock...to the YRBM 16, three times a day, where we showered, ate our meals, and relaxed.

The South Vietnamese Army soldiers...manned their boats every evening...to go on night patrols along the

Vinh Te canal. They would set up camps along the canal to ambush the North Vietnamese Army soldiers...who were sneaking into South Vietnam over the Cambodian border...during the night.

After a few months of living on our dock, our unit was moved into the YRBM 20. It was about a mile down the river from the YRBM 16.

Our ski boats were all driven down to the YRBM 20...where they waited for our floating dock to be moved there, also. Once the dock was secured to the YRBM 20, our ski boats were tied up to the dock again.

We were given a living space in the YRBM 20. After living on the floating dock for a few months, this seemed like a floating hotel to us. The living conditions were much better.

Up to that point, everything was going according to schedule. I felt good...being a part of a team of dedicated sailors...with a cause...and a purpose.

We worked all day...repairing our boats, and then we had our evenings free. We had great meals, with a variety of good food. We were working together as a team, and everyone was getting along.

The only bad thing that happened to me during that time, was the 'Dear John letter', that I received in the mail...from the girl back home...that I thought I was going to marry.

The day that I received that letter...was the second worse day...of my stay in Vietnam. That, in itself, could have caused my PTSD. But, I survived and life went on.

I did several things to keep myself busy in the evening. I started learning to play the guitar from a couple of the guys I worked with. This went well. I learned to play a lot of chords and several songs.

A few of us...lifted weights every day after work to beat down the stress of our job. We always started our workout by doing 100 pushups. Sometimes, after the workout...we would do another 100.

After our evening workouts, I would spend the rest of the night...writing letters to everyone I knew...back in the states.

In November, I started buying Christmas presents, for everyone in my family...and all the members of three other families. That totaled about 15 people. I bought the presents in Chao Doc...at the local marketplace. I would buy and mail all the presents for one family at the same time. I had all the presents mailed by...December 15th.

All of these things kept me busy and engaged in worthwhile activities.

During December...our combat mission became very critical. The crossing of the North Vietnamese soldiers...over the Cambodian border...into South

Vietnam...had increased in frequently and numbers.

The attacks on our military bases in the area...were also increasing.

Because of that, our workload dramatically increased, also. Our work schedule increased from eight hours a day...to 10 to 12 hours a day...seven days a week.

The more our ski boats went on patrol...the more damage was done to them.

Along with the increase in our workload...another problem had begun. The Monsoon season was over and the temperatures had begun to rise.

In the next few months, the average daily temperature rose to 115 degrees, with 90% humidity. The dock, that our ski boats were moored to...and that our workstation was on...was a hollow metal container, about 100 feet by 50 feet.

The hollow area inside the container...from the deck to the floor was about 5 feet deep.

When the temperature got up to 120 degrees...with 90% humidity...the hollow area inside of the metal barge...would fill up with heat. The heat would turn to steam and rise through the deck...that we were working on. Sometimes, the deck we were working on...would get up to 135 degrees. Add to that, 90% humidity, and it would become suffocating.

Because our work was critical to the success of the

South Vietnamese mission on the canal, we would work most of those days. Once-in-awhile...our supervisors...who were drinking coffee, in the cafeteria, would let us knock off for the afternoon.

We were working seven days a week through December and January.

Christmas Day was a few days away...and they told us that we had to work that day also.

Due to the stress of the job, my patience was wearing very thin. The other guys in the unit were as frustrated as I was.

We talked about what we could do to...and we decided to take the day off and go into town. We had to have a good excuse to do that, so we decided that going to visit an orphanage in town...with some Christmas presents...seemed to be a good enough reason for us.

So, instead of getting up and working...on Christmas Day, we got into one of our boats and drove into Chau Doc and visited an orphanage.

We caught hell for doing that, but it was worth it.

That is when my attitude of teamwork and co-operations...started to change. I was taught that to get respect, you had to give respect.

We were not getting any respect from our supervisors, so I felt...I no longer had to give them any respect.

This was the beginning of my demise...as a good sailor.

One of the major work-related problems...we were having...was getting parts...to repair the outboard engines that powered the ski boats. Each of the 50 boats had two 60-horsepower Johnson outboard engines attached to them.

The boats had been on the canal...for several months now...and the parts in the outboard engines, were wearing out. Some due to normal wear and tear – others...due to the abuse the soldiers driving the boats were giving them.

When we began to run out of spare parts, we would give a list of parts that we needed to our supervisors. After a month...of not getting any replacement parts...we began to ask more aggressively...and not so politely...why we were not getting the essential parts that we needed to keep the boats on the river.

They would tell us that they were doing the best they could...to get us the spare parts, and for us to get back to work.

After a while, we were so frustrated with not being able to fix the outboard motors...on the boats, that a few of us, got together to discuss how we could best solve our problem. We decided that our supervisors were really lying to us about not being able to get the parts...because they were just too lazy to order them.

I don't know if this was true or not...but with our limited view of how the supply chain...in a war operated, we decided it probably was true.

Because, we were trying to repair motors with limited spare parts...we could not do our jobs effectively. We felt frustrated, lonely, and abandoned.

We were supposed to be supporting the South Vietnamese soldiers, who were fighting the Viet Cong...and trying to win this war. We felt like we weren't doing all that we could do...to support them...which was the mission we were given.

The only recourse that I could see...was to fight back against those who were putting me in this untenable situation. They were making it impossible for us to succeed in our assigned mission.

My frustration was building...to the point...that I began to get angry...with my supervisors. I felt like I was expressing my anger in an appropriate manner. But it wasn't getting me anywhere. As a result, I began to despise them for being so incompetent...in this combat situation.

As time went on, my hostility and anger turned to hate.

When the Vietnamese smashed up the boats, which they did every day going to and from their patrols, or when the outboard motors broke down, our job was to fix them.

These ski boats had two outboard motors on each boat, and therefore were very powerful. The South Vietnamese soldiers were not used to driving such powerful boats, so they had trouble controlling them, as they drove up and down the canal.

When they were on the canal, the driver of a boat, would play with the other boats driving along side of his boat. Sometimes they would crash into another boat while they were playing around with or lose control of their boat and run up on the canal bank and hit a tree.

The Viet Cong also did damage to the boats. As the boats were cruising up and down the canal, the Viet Cong would fire rockets and mortars into the boats sometimes sinking them.

Every night that the South Vietnamese soldiers went out on patrol, one or two of us, from our unit, would go with them. We went along to take care of any problems the boats might be having.

At least that is the argument, that we used to talk our Lieutenant into letting us ride along on the night patrols. He didn't want us anywhere near the enemy, so he said we couldn't go out on the patrols.

After weeks of being persistent, we finally convinced him, that we really could help the South Vietnamese army soldiers deal with some of the problems they were having getting the boats back to the base, after their night patrols.

For example, if an outboard motor stopped working, they would need a mechanic to get it running again. If two boats ran into each other, we could help get the boats apart and keep them afloat long enough to get back to the base.

That is how we convinced him to let us go on night patrols. The real reason was because we wanted to see some real combat action. Also, we thought it would be cool to see our soldiers fight the enemy.

One night, I got my turn to go on this long-awaited night-out with the boys. My hope was, (as was the hope of all of the guys in my unit), that I would see some real combat.

Once my turn came to go out on a night patrol with the South Vietnamese soldiers, and...I realized that I was really going out on a combat mission to engage the enemy, I was super excited.

Then, when I thought about it and I realized that it really was a combat mission, I was super scared. I was actually going out on night patrol with real army men.

I say real army men, because as a child, I grew up playing cowboys and Indians with all my neighborhood friends.

Around eight years old, I started playing with plastic army men. My friends and I created life-like battle scenarios...like the ones we had seen on TV, and the movies.

Around the age of 12, I started my own Army Club, with a couple of my neighborhood friends.

To help us look like real soldiers, we went to the local Army Surplus store and bought helmets...army belts...combat boots...and any other army paraphernalia, that would make us look like real army men in our backyard battles.

We even cut guns, out of wood, that we picked out of the dumpster from a lumber mill close to our house.

Then one day, we got really brave and decided to go to a Military recruiter's office downtown. I don't remember what we thought we would accomplish by doing that, but it sounded like it would be fun.

The first place we went was to the Army recruiter's office. He wouldn't even talk to us...so we went next door to the Marine recruiter's office. He seemed excited to see us. He asked us to come into his office...and he talked to us for a while.

He was so impressed with our desire to join the Marines, which is what we told him, that he gave us a couple of his old Marine uniforms for our club. Of course, we wore them around our backyards proudly, as we shot at each other with our wooden guns.

Those were the fantasies about war that I had as a child and teenager.

Now, I was in Vietnam. It wasn't a fantasy any longer. I was about to go into a real battle, against a real enemy, with real guns and bullets.

I really did not have a clue, as to what a real battle looked like.

But...now it was my turn to go into battle, with the South Vietnam soldiers.

I was going to go out on a night patrol, with a unit of South Vietnamese Army to fight the enemy.

The full unit that I was going out with...on this night patrol, consisted of 30 ski boats, each with a 50-caliber machine gun mounted on the bow. The boats were manned by 50 South Vietnamese soldiers, with me, and one other sailor from my KSB unit going with them.

All of the boats, in our unit, left for the canal...early in the evening. The unit was divided into groups...that consisted of two boats, with four soldiers in each boat.

Each group was assigned a spot on the canal to set up their ambush.

North Vietnamese soldiers would be coming across the canal into South Vietnam from Cambodia during the night.

The South Vietnamese soldiers would be spread out along the canal. That was because the NVA soldiers always crossed the canal in a different place each night.

So, each group of South Vietnamese soldiers...who had set up an ambush spot on the canal...had no idea if they would make contact that night with the enemy or not.

Two South Vietnamese soldiers in each group, would take 4-hour shifts staying awake during the night...to watch for any enemy troops that might be trying to cross the canal at their location.

I was assigned to one of the groups of South Vietnamese soldiers. My assignment was to help with any possible mechanical problems on way... to or from...the canal, for the whole group of 30 boats.

The designated spot...to set up an ambush for my group, was next to a small village of Vietnamese families. The village consisted of 10 to 15 huts, on both sides of the canal.

American soldiers nicknamed the huts, hootches. The hootches were made out of wood and straw. They were about 15 ft. by 15 ft. They consisted of one room...with each hootch having a bed or two, a chair, and something like a rug to cover the dirt floor.

When my group of soldiers, got to our ambush spot, we unloaded our boats and set up our camp for the night. When I say, set up our camp...I mean we each picked a spot to sleep and laid out gear and rifles next to it.

By the time we got all our gear laid out, it was just getting dark. One of the local Vietnamese...talked to the soldier in charge of our group...and he invited my whole group to have dinner with him...in his hootch.

There were nine of us in my group. The hootch...including the front door...was so small, I had to duck to get into it. It had 1 room with a bed, chair, and a 5 ft, by 5-ft rug, in the middle of a dirt floor. We all sat down around the rug.

Our host...brought out our food in several bowls...and put the bowls in the center of the rug. We were each given an empty bowl, with some chopsticks.

The way the meals were eaten there, was that each of us would take a bowl of food...from the center of the rug...dish some of it into their bowl and eat it.

When we had eaten all the food in our bowl, we would dish some food from another bowl, in the center of the rug. There were several types of vegetable, fish, and meat in the bowls. Everyone around the rug served themselves, until the food was all gone.

I ate my food using the chopsticks. The Vietnamese were very impressed that I even knew how to use chopsticks.

I learned how to use chopsticks back in Eugene, Oregon, where I grew up. My church group consisted of about five of us teenagers...around the same age. We would go out for dinner on Sundays...to a local Chinese restaurant. We would have a contest to see who could eat their meal using just the chopsticks. The first one to use a fork...had to pay for someone else's meal.

When our meal in the hootch was done...one of the guys brought out a bottle of Vietnamese whiskey called 'Basade'. Then...he passed out a shot glass to everyone.

I couldn't believe...that in that remote part of the world...with primitive huts... they had shot glasses.

Anyway, everyone in the circle was poured a drink.

Because I did not drink alcohol, I refused my glass of Basade. Our Vietnamese host kept insisting...that I let him fill my glass. I finally gave in.

So, there I was...sitting there...with a shot glass of liquor in my hand...looking around...at all the Vietnamese staring at me. They were waiting to see if I would drink it or not. I was the only American within 50 miles, in a hostile place, and everyone in the room had a gun, so I agreed to take the drink.

As I swallowed it, it burned all the way down...from my throat to my stomach. I started coughing and coughing. Everyone started pointing at me and laughing.

Up to that time in my life, I had not drunk a full glass of alcohol. I did take a sip of beer...with some guys I went out to a party with...from high school, but I spit it out because it tasted like piss to me.

So, drinking that glass of whiskey in that Vietnamese hootch for the first time, was a shock to my system.

I thought that that excruciating episode was over, but it wasn't. About 15 minutes later, one of the neighboring Vietnamese guys...came to the door.

They started talking to him in Vietnamese...so, I didn't know what they were saying. All of a sudden, someone pulled out a shot glass, filled it with whiskey and handed it to me and said, 'drink'.

I realized then that I was the entertainment for the night. I drank it and coughed and coughed. They all laughed and laughed.

So...after dinner, we went to our ambush spot and got ready for the action that we were expecting.

I had an M-16 machine rifle with me, as well as a 45-pistol, in a holster and belt, that I had around my waste. I also had a steel helmet and a bulletproof flak jacket.

They weren't expecting to make contact with any of the enemy...until the middle of the night. So...I took off all my gear, laid down, put my head on my helmet, and went to sleep.

Around 1:00 AM, I woke up to a lot of gunshots going off around me. My instincts immediately kicked in and I knew exactly what I was supposed to do.

The first thing I did was to put on my bulletproof flak jacket, then I grabbed my helmet and put it on. I also had a steel helmet, that went on top of my regular helmet, to make sure a bullet didn't go into my head.

Next, I picked up my 45 pistol and strapped the holster around my waist. After grabbing my M-16 automatic rifle off the ground, I looked around to see what was going on.

I was standing next to a small hill...that was about 10 ft high. On the top of the hill...two South Vietnamese soldiers were shooting at something in the canal. The beginning of the canal was about 15 feet in front of me.

By now I was a 100% in the 'fight or flight' mode. I was ready for action. This was my chance to fight in a real war, with a real enemy. As I ran through the options in my mind...I decided that I would go up on the hill, where the other soldiers were, and shoot at whoever, or whatever, they were shooting at.

I took two steps towards them and my whole body froze. I realized, for the first time...since me and the guys in my unit, had started talking about being in combat, that if...I went up on that hill...I could be killed.

When that realization hit me, my whole body was consumed with fear. I was paralyzed by the fear... that what I never thought would happen, was...about to happen.

I just stood there, like a statue. I could not move a muscle. I did not want to die, or get wounded, or even get shot, so I froze.

That was the moment my PTSD happened.

After a few minutes of standing there immobile, I finally decided that I had to do something, because I couldn't just stand there.

So, I decided that I would just stay where I was standing.

I was not going to go up on that hill. So...I took a couple of steps towards the canal and looked around for something to shoot at.

All the action was in front of me and to the right of me. No one seemed to be shooting to my left. I didn't know why...no one was shooting in that area, so I decided that I would shoot over there, just in case some of the enemy was in that area.

After about 15 minutes, the shooting was over. Then everyone calmed down.

Because, no one was asking me to do anything, I took off my helmet, and my flax jacket. I took of my 45-pistol, laid that and my M-16 on the ground, laid my head on my helmet and went back to sleep.

The same thing happened again towards the morning...but by the time I had gotten all my gear on, the shooting had stopped.

In the morning, there were two dead NVA soldiers in the canal. They were carrying large black plastic garbage bags, full of clothes, ammo, and medical supplies. We spread the items in their packs, out on the ground, so we could inventory the contents.

Later that morning, the South Vietnamese soldier in charge of our patrol, came over to me, and told me that someone in the village, on the other side of the canal, wanted to talk to me.

I was the only American anywhere around...and I was not in charge of anything, so I couldn't figure out why...anyone over there, wanted to talk to me.

Then I realized that there were about ten hootches across the canal to the left of our ambush area.

I was again struck with a paralyzing fear. I realized, that during the ambush, when I shot to my left, it was into that village. Still not knowing why I was being called to the village, I reluctantly got into a boat and went across the canal to the village, on the other side.

When I got to the village, my guide took me...up to a little old Vietnamese lady, that was screaming her head off, and pointing to a 3 ft tall vase in front of her small hooch. The vase had a bullet hole right through the middle of it.

She was yelling in Vietnamese, which I didn't speak, so I just stood there and looked dumb, which I was. I was hoping I wasn't the one who shot her vase, and I was really hoping that there wasn't a dead body inside the hootch.

To my relief, no one was injured by my bullet. But...I am sure that she wanted someone to replace her vase. After a heated discussion, we left the village, packed up the dead NVA soldiers, and rode the ski boats back to the barge we were living on...about 20 miles away.

War is the most destructive and pitiless of all human activities. And yet the experience of war has a profound...and strangely compelling effect on those who are in combat.

Combat kills, maims, and terrifies...but, it also can reveal the power of brotherhood and a self-less sense of purpose.

That last statement is why I put so much of my energy and passion into the Vietnam war. The article said...that combat has a self-less sense of purpose and a powerful brotherhood.

Those two things, a self-less sense of purpose and a powerful brotherhood, were the same standards that I...was raised by.

The most important thing in my life growing up was my church.

My church taught us that the highest qualities in life were...putting others before yourself...and being of service to your fellowmen.

That is what war is. When a soldier goes into battle, they are going to have one of three dominant attitudes.

The first...is that they are going to feel like and believe that they are the baddest beast in the jungle...and I can kill anyone who gets in my way.

The second attitude is...that they were sent to fight...by people they don't even know and they will do their best to stay alive.

The third is...that they feel obligated to protect the people they love, and they will do anything to do that...even die for them.

My attitude towards the war in Vietnam was the third. I volunteered to go to Vietnam to fight the war.

I grew up in an extremely patriotic family. My dad had served in Europe in WWII.

My church taught me that America was the land of the free...and that God had inspired the Unites States constitution. The Constitutions purpose was to preserve our freedoms.

I believed what my family and my church taught me.

It was my feeling of patriotism towards my country, my desire to defend my country, and my desire to protect my family and friends...that motivated me to volunteer to go fight in Vietnam.

I made the decision to volunteer to be transferred to Vietnam...when I was floating in the Pacific Ocean, on the USS Maddox. My ship was about 100 miles off the shore of Long Beach, California.

I was standing on the bow of the ship, leaning on the railing, and looking out over an empty ocean.

I thought to myself, "I am here, on this ship, doing very little to help my country...and 8,000 miles away in Vietnam...there are soldiers and sailors, just like me, fighting and dying for their country. What...am I doing here? I should be there"?

That is when...I went to the personnel office on my ship and told them that I wanted to volunteer to go to Vietnam.

They looked at me a little weird...but they said that they could make it happen.

Most of the sailors in the Navy...were looking for ways to stay as far away from Vietnam as possible. I was asking to be put in the middle of a combat zone.

Only 25% of the Navy served in Vietnam...and most of them were not there by choice.

Was it because of foolishness, or insanity that I listened to the voice in my head that told me to volunteer to go to Vietnam? I don't know which one it was. It was probably, just because I was very naïve about how that single decision would change my life.

Although I had the best of intentions...in hindsight...that decision did not turn out to be the best thing for me.

The attitudes of patriotism, selflessness, and service to others, that my family and church had taught me...were the reasons that I volunteered to go to Vietnam...and were the dominate attitudes that caused me to put my whole heart and soul into fighting in that war.

Just like I put so much energy and passion in my church service during my teenage years...in Vietnam...I put the same amount of energy, passion, and service into trying to be the best sailor I could be.

This is what happened to me...at that moment. My brain went into the 'fight or flight' mode, where my emotions were blunted as a defense mechanism to protect me...from the bullets...that were flying all around me.

That sounds good, you may be saying...so...what's the problem.

The problem for me is that at that moment... my brain was locked into the 'fight or flight' mode and...I have never gotten out of it.

The result of that is...that for my whole life since then, I have felt very little emotion. My emotional self, my passion, my intensity...has been turned off.

I still had the desire to accomplish my goals and persuade my friends and co-workers...that my point of view was the right one...but instead of passion, I used aggression and hostility. It still felt like passion to me, but it felt very different to the person or person's...I was focusing my aggression on.

My aggression was not fueled with the emotional desire to help myself...or my friends...it was fueled by the desire to win...and I used aggression and intimidation to cause the other person to want to back off and get out of there.

'Didn't I see that I was causing contention and chaos with the other person? ...you may ask.

The answer to that is a resounding 'No'. If I did not have any emotions in the discussion, I didn't think the other person did either. In other words, I couldn't read their body language to see that I was causing them pain and discomfort.

Add 'hatred', the dominant emotion I was constantly feeling, and I became a very hostile, combative, and belligerent person. Not a good way to 'make friends and influence people', even though...I had read the book.

My next 2 ½ years in the Navy, fed my hatred for all things military. I became very adept at using it...to win any argument. I could become the center of attention by turning on the hatred inside me...and letting it out into the room. Because, the people I was with...had never felt that kind of emotional intensity, they usually backed away from it.

When I was confronted with the same intensity that I was showing, the battle for control was on. The adrenaline would start pumping in me and it felt good.

Now, I knew I would win, because I was the baddest beast in the valley. If I lost, that was OK, because the battle was worth it.

When I looked at everyone as the enemy, who is trying to stop me from my goal...and I added the emotion of hatred to it...then I became an immovable force...that reeks destruction in its path.

During my stay in Vietnam and for the rest of my time in the Navy, that is what I became.

My goal in life was to dominate through intimidation and fear. I usually won the battle, because, I put so much aggressive emotion into it.

Intense hatred is as powerful, and as intense as love. We all know how much good can happen, when love is the motiving factor.

But, I would guess...that there are only a few of us who know how much destruction can be caused...when hatred is the power behind the actions.

After Vietnam, my battles turned from physical ones to verbal battles. In the verbal battles I fought and won, I was usually the one that could display the most intense hatred.

My verbal battles were aimed at those trying to stop me from reaching whatever my goal was at the time. It didn't matter who they were, or what position they held above me.

I became an immovable force, an unmanageable employee, a lousy friend, and a non-sympathetic and empathetic person. In my mind, I ruled, period!

It was not just the classic, 'my way…or the highway', it was, 'my way…or go to hell'.

My mantra became, "Yea, though I walk through the valley of the shadow of death, I will fear no evil, for I am the baddest beast in the jungle".

That hatred lived inside me for about 10 years after I was discharged from the Navy.

I eventually realized how much destruction, that single emotion, was causing in my life…and I found ways to extinguish it.

Even when the hatred was gone, the attitudes and habits that my hatred had created in me, stayed with me for most of my life. Some still determine my behavior today.

In an article on hatred…People also hate…when they feel powerless. Rather than turning their anxiety and shame inward…they may project that negativity onto an external target.

In some cases, people who experience bullying or abuse may grow to hate the person who harmed them.

This explains why I began to 'hate' my supervisors. I felt like, I was powerless to stop them from hurting me.

I did not realize that my hurt was internal (on me) and not external (on my supervisors). And...that the cause of my anxiety was the fact...I that **was not able to do my job...and I was feeling shame, because I felt like I was a failure. That, also,** was totally my problem, not my supervisors.

Instead of trying to solve the problem with the options that were available...or accepting that the problem could not be solved, **I blamed my supervisors.**

I should have just accepted that this was as good as it got and moved on.

In other cases, the target of a person's hatred... is hated more for what they represent than for the specific actions they have taken against that person.

Individuals...may believe the target of their hatred has ...harmful intentions toward them...and would hurt them, if they could.

However, the person they see as the target...may not necessarily have hostile intentions towards that person...or the hatred may be disproportional to the injury.

In my case, the target of my hatred was...my supervisors. I really didn't hate them...because they didn't do anything to me, directly. But, they represented the Navy, who did have power over me. The Navy had put me in the middle of the war in Vietnam. The Navy and the war were who...I was really mad at.

They are the ones that put me in this situation...where I was literally being hurt...physically, mentally, and emotionally.

But...I was stuck in Vietnam for a year...and that was not going to change. The war was going to continue...no matter what I did...and neither of those things were going to change.

Because I felt helpless to have any impact on either of those things...I focused my hatred on the closest thing to me that I had any effect on...and that was my supervisors.

As the article said: they may not necessarily...have had hostile intentions towards me, and the hatred that I turned on them...may have been disproportional to the injury that I felt they had caused me. That injury, in my case, was my feeling of utter helplessness.

This feeling of helplessness is what caused so much fear in me...that my brain felt justified in switching from its normal functions...to the 'fight or flight' mode to protect me.

So, in hindsight, 50 years later, I can see that my disrespect, and sometimes my outright disobedience, towards my supervisors, was the wrong thing to do.

I can see now that the 2nd class Petty Officer and the Lieutenant, who were my bosses, were not out to purposely hurt, or to destroy me. They were just doing the jobs that they were supposed to do.

The fact that they were causing me so much anxiety and pain...was not their goal, it was just a result of doing their jobs.

The article goes on to say: (quote) For example, a student may hate a teacher who failed them in a class. The teacher may not have any hostility for the student and could simply be doing their job. However, the student may use the teacher as a stand-in for their frustration with academia as a whole.

This hatred may prompt the student to try and harm the teacher, perhaps by spreading false rumors or sending a vicious email.

Studies on hatred suggest...that if the hatred persists, prolonged hatred may lead to a desire for revenge or preemptive action against a perceived threat.

Some people harbor hatred for others...but never act on it. Others become energized by hate and express their feelings through <u>violent acts</u>.

Feelings of hatred that develop toward a certain individual...may eventually be redirected toward the entire group that person belongs to. This can lead to dehumanization of individuals or groups.

Dehumanization is the act of seeing a person as inferior, uncivilized, or less than human.

Dehumanization research suggests that when people see others, as less than human, the <u>empathy that</u> centers in the brain is deactivated.

For example, people who commit <u>violence</u>, cruelty, or hate crimes often rationalize these actions...by comparing the victims to animals. Individuals who would typically balk at murdering another person...may find it easier to kill a "subhuman" enemy. (unquote)

Let's break down these last few paragraphs.

The article says that a student may hate a teacher who failed them in a class. The teacher may not have felt any hostility toward the student...and could simply be doing their job.

However, the student may use the teacher as a stand-in for their frustration with academia as a whole.

As I just explained, that is what I did. I saw my supervisors as my enemy. They were causing my problems. In reality, they had nothing to do with my problems.

The Navy and the war were creating my problems. My supervisors had no effect on what the Navy did...and they had no effect on how the war was negatively affecting me.

But, as the article said, my hatred prompted me to try to harm my supervisors.

I couldn't do anything physically to harm them, or I would have been thrown in the brig. That...was never an option for me...so I had to figure some other way to get to them.

What I settled on was rebellion, disobedience, and verbal abuse.

For the rest of my Navy career, I rebelled against everything I was told to do by my supervisors. Again, I didn't do anything physical, just verbal abuse.

If they told me to repair an engine part...I told them I didn't know how to do that particular repair, and therefore, I couldn't be trusted to do it. I told them that if I watched someone else do it one time, I might know how to do it the next time.

Then...when the next time rolled around, I used a

similar excuse.

I told my supervisors...that I was so incompetent...so many times over the next few years, that they quit asking me to anything on my own.

In private...with my co-workers, I questioned everything we were told to do.   I didn't say that we shouldn't do it, I just said it was unnecessary...that we do it right now, and that we should do it later.

I was very effective in getting my co-workers to work slower than our supervisors wanted us to.

This was another way I rebelled against authority.

In doing this, my disrespect for all authority grew and grew...until it became the dominant attitude that I had toward any supervisor that I worked for from then on, either in the military, in the business world, or in my church.

My attitude of disrespect was ingrained in me because of my hatred towards my supervisors in Vietnam. Once I was out of Vietnam, and in a non-hostile workplace, I still couldn't get rid of that attitude of disrespecting authority.

The hatred that I felt for my supervisors in Vietnam, the Navy, and the war...faded away after five to ten years in civilian life. Once it became manageable, I was able to get rid of it completely.

But...the habits that I had developed...from the years of rebelling against authority, such as, talking trash about my managers...and outright disobeying them...I could not get rid of.

Those habits, just like any habit, became a part of me. They had been with me for so long and were so useful in helping me to get what I wanted, that I could not see how destructive and rebellious they were in my civilian life.

They had served a purpose when I was in the Navy, but those attitudes had no place in civilian life.

Even though, I developed those attitudes in 1970, I did not realize that they were a liability to me...until a few years ago.

As a result, over the years, I have never been successful in a management position. I have always been...the unmanageable employee, who you left alone to do his job.

This is the damage PTSD can do in a person's life, even over a lifetime. PTSD changes the brain and develops attitudes the person needed...at the time of the traumatic event, to survive...but become detrimental to that person in normal social situations. Sometimes, years after that traumatic event is over, those same attitudes are still there.

Over time, they seem normal to the person, even though they are destructive in every aspect of that person's life and relationships.

Now, I am not just talking about what I think happens as a result of PTSD, I am telling you what happened to me. To me...these symptoms of PTSD are real, even if...they have not been documented by some research study.

It wasn't until 1998...when I finally agreed to go see a Vietnam Veteran's counselor, that I began to see how my out-of-whack and destructive attitudes...that I had created in 1970...had been hurting my relationships in all areas of my life since then.

My counselor showed me what PTSD was...how I was suffering from the symptoms of PTSD...and how my life could be much better if I got some counseling to learn how to deal with them.

I want to change directions for a minute or so. I want to tell you about another **epiphany that I have had about another one of the symptoms of my PTSD.**

I have been hyper-active...since I was in my 20's...but I thought the reason was that I had ADHD. I have known several people with ADHD...and their symptoms looked like my hyper-activity.

But, I was tested for ADHD a few years ago, and the evaluator said I did not have enough symptoms to qualify for that disorder. I have a friend who has been diagnosed with PTSD and I even took a couple his Adderall pills. They had slowed down his hyper-activity, but they didn't have any effect on me.

The research I did...showed me that my hyper-activity was a result of my PTSD.

My hyper-activity began when my brain changed from a normal function...to the 'Fight or Flight' mode...during the firefight in Vietnam.

Numbed emotions, and dehumanizing people...describes two of the PTSD symptoms, that I have....Per an article I read on my podcast.

Now, I can see how it is so easy for me to manipulate people, without any regard for their feelings.

This is what the article says:

(quote) Feelings of hatred that develop toward a certain individual may eventually be redirected toward the entire group that person belongs to. This can lead to dehumanization of individuals or groups. Dehumanization is the act of seeing a person as inferior, uncivilized, or less than human.

Dehumanization research suggests that when people see others, as less than human, the **empathy that centers in the brain is deactivated.** (unquote)

My epiphany was...that I finally understood what had caused me to ignore the orders my superiors were giving me. That includes...my supervisors in Vietnam...and all my supervisors and managers since then.

My PTSD had caused the empathy part of my brain...to be deactivated. Because of that...I started seeing any supervisor as non-human. Not that they weren't people...they just weren't people with feelings, that I had to take into consideration, when I was manipulating them to get them to do what I wanted them to.

I looked at them the same way I would look at an object. When I would look at an object, I would ask, "what can this object do for me. The object had no feelings, so it doesn't matter what I do to it. I can use it anyway I need to, in order to accomplish my goals." That is how I dehumanized my superiors.

Also, I now realize what my numbed emotions were. I had always divided people that I was working with...into 2 groups. The first group is the people that agree with my goals and will help me accomplish them. These are people that I can manipulate to get what I want.

The second group...is the people who do not agree with me. They are the ones...who are trying to keep me from reaching my goal. I look at these people as non-people, or people who just aren't important to my goals.

My goal is to manipulate both groups into doing things my way. The group that is sympathetic to me is easy to manipulate. They are the useful objects.

If they are not on my side, or I cannot control them, then I will simply discard, or ignore them.

This is the reason I have not been able to connect with people...and why I cannot sympathize or empathize with anyone.

I can understand how people feel, but that only matters to me, if I can use them to get what I want.

I am sure you don't understand how I can do this...so let me use the analogy of a chess game to explain it.

When I set a goal and want to get people on my side, I set up a chess board in my mind. There are the pieces that are on my side, that I can use, and there are pieces that are on the other side, and they are the ones that are against me.

In this game...the chess pieces are real people...but I don't see them that way.

To me they are just objects, to be manipulated. If I see them as real people, I will not be able to use them...like I need to.

In order to accomplish my goals, I need to move my pieces where they can effectively beat the enemy.

As I play the game, I need to capture, or disable the enemy pieces...so that they can't stop me from meeting my objective...which is to win the game.

Achieving my goal, is equivalent to checkmating the opposing King. To do that, I have to trap or capture all the Kings pieces on the board.

This is the definition of dehumanizing a person or group of people.

What happens to the chessmen...or the real people I am working with, or against...does not matter to me. All that matters to me is that I accomplish my goal, which is to win the game.

If I sympathize, or empathize with the opposing pieces on the board, these positive emotional feelings might keep me from making some moves that will help me win the game.

For example, I could use my knight to take my opponent's pawn. That would put me in a position to take my opponents Bishop.

But, if I really like my knight, I may not feel like sacrificing him. Then, I may not make the move...and that might leave my King open to an attack.

These positive emotional feelings play a role in all of our relationships. We want to protect the people we love...and have empathy for...and we do not want to see them get hurt.

In order to win in chess, all the pieces have to do what I want them to. I can't be concerned about how the pieces...either mine or the opponents...might feel about the move I am going to make. My only concern can be...my desire to win and to achieve my goal.

In my world, feelings for my own men...or the opposing men...have no place in my battle strategy. Maybe I might care what is best for them...but I care more about what is best for me.

If I add a negative emotion to the mix...like hate...then that emotion motivates me even more to protect the ones I love...and destroy the ones who are trying to hurt them. Just like in war. Protect the ones you love and kill the ones you hate.

You may feel like asking me, "why don't I just change, when I realize that trying to accomplish my objective...is hurting the other people".

Let me answer that this way. In the game of chess, I don't care if I am hurting the pieces on my chess board. The object of the game is to win. That is all that matters. I use all the pieces to accomplish my goal. They have no feelings and I have no feeling towards them.

It is not...that I don't want to feel other people's pain...it is that the part of my brain that helps me see how they feel, doesn't work. I really can't feel what they are feeling. My brain isn't allowing me to.

In my case, the empathy part of my brain, stopped working when my brain went into the 'Fight or Flight' mode after the firefight in Vietnam.

Not only did it stop working, but, I didn't know...that it had stopped working. All of a sudden, it just wasn't there. I couldn't start something up again...if I didn't know it had stopped.

It wasn't until 1998, 28 years after my PTSD event, that my Vietnam Veterans counselor showed me what PTSD was...and how it had affected other Vietnam Veterans. As I watched videos of the symptoms of their PTSD, I saw the same symptoms in myself.

That is when I could see how much my manipulative actions were hurting other people. That is when my brain began to move from the 'Fight or Flight' mode to the normal mode.

But, even though I could see that, it still took 10 more years for me to complete the transition back to the normal part of my brain.

In my personal experience, in trying to manage my own PTSD for 50 years, I found that I was the only one that could reprogram my dysfunctional brain to become normal again. I was lucky enough to have two very good therapists, that opened some doors for me, so I could make that change, and a few people close to me that helped me immensely.

Those 2 therapists...and a few other people very close to me...have been the reason that now, I can calmly...describe how my PTSD has screwed up my life and my relationships and talk to you about it.

Just the fact, that I can describe to you...how my PTSD has caused so many dysfunctions in my life, means that I am talking to you now...from the normal part of my brain, and not the dysfunctional PTSD part.

If there is an extremely traumatic event during a temporary situation...that causes you to have PTSD, then it is possible that your temporary personality...at the time of the event...can be cemented or locked into your brain functions. Once this change takes place, it may take years for you to unlock your brain, so you can return to your normal self, again.

This is what I did in Vietnam. Before I went to Vietnam, I was a mild-mannered, easy-going person. I got along with everyone, and for the most part...I was well liked.

My experiences in Vietnam, caused me to become a very angry, hostile, and combative person in order to protect myself from what I perceived as abuse from my superiors.

So, when my PTSD event happened...the personality that was locked or cemented in for the rest of my life, was not the submissive personality that I had before I went to Vietnam, it was the angry, hostile, and combative personality that I had recently developed in Vietnam.

As I have told you, I was mild-mannered and respectful as a teenager. Most of my attitudes and behaviors were pretty normal and socially acceptable.

Most people's attitudes and behaviors change slightly, as they grow older.

My personality, attitudes, and behaviors changed drastically, when I went into the Navy.

And they changed even more drastically in Vietnam.

So, why didn't I go back to my mild-mannered personality that I had as a teenager, when I got out of the Navy? The forces that had caused me to change my personality, were no longer there. But, I still kept that personality, with all my new and dysfunctional attitudes and behaviors for the rest of my life.

Now I can see that the reason I didn't go back to the nicer me, was because my brain had changed from its normal functions to the 'fight or flight' functions...that were dysfunctional. I couldn't change it back, because I didn't know that it had changed. I wasn't controlling my brain; my brain was controlling me...and I didn't even know it.

This describes exactly how I felt during the firefight that I was in, in Vietnam.

The increase in my **adrenaline flow**...that caused my

pulse and blood pressure levels to dramatically increase...was such a rush to my heart, brain, and major muscle groups...that I tried for years after that to put myself in situations...where those sensations could be replicated.

But, for the rest of my life, I never found a single event that was as 'insanely exciting'. The reason for that is because in my middle-income life and my stable environment, there are no experiences that rose to that level of fear and excitement.

That's not to say...that I didn't try to recreate that level of excitement, because I did...repeatedly.

But, because I didn't have a gun, or an enemy to shoot at...in my daily life, it was impossible to get that excessive level of adrenaline that I had experienced in the firefight.

I did continually try to re-create situations where I would get a good rush of adrenaline.

My disrespect for authority and my need to argue and debate were the tools I used to get that rush. You could say that those were my drugs of choice.

While I was in Vietnam...disobeying the orders of my supervisors...was the only thing that could get my adrenaline flowing like it did in the firefight.

If my adrenaline flow in the firefight was a 10, then whenever I blatantly disobeyed my supervisors in

Vietnam, it was about a five.

To put that in perspective, when I did obey something, one of my supervisors told me to do...and I just went along to get along with whatever we were doing, that would rate as a two on my adrenaline rush scale.

The reason disobeying orders rated a five...was because, when I didn't do what I was told to do, by someone who had a higher rank than I did...it really ticked them off. When they got mad at me, (which they always did), then I got just as mad at them.

When they told me that I had to obey an order they gave me, I politely told them 'to make me'.

This is where my verbal superiority came in. I was better at debating them...than they were at getting me to obey them.

When I was arguing with them...about something they had told me to do, I would raise my voice and look and sound as intimidating as I could. I would also use 50 cent words, that they were usually not familiar with.

What made them so mad was that I was not acting according to Navy protocol. Navy protocol dictated that when a person above me in rank, gave me an order...I would unquestionably execute it.

I never did that. I always had some reason that I couldn't do what I was told to do. I stated my reasons for non-compliance with forcefulness, with an air of superiority. Because they were so used to everyone just doing what they told them to do, they didn't know how to react to me. I was a true anomaly to them.

When a sailor would get in their face, or disobey them, when they gave him an order, they would write him up and send him to see the captain of the ship. This was called a Captain's Mast. The captain gives them a punishment...like making them stay on the ship for a week or two... bust them down a rank...or put them in the brig.

My goal was never to be sent to a captain's mast. So, I would increase my belligerence towards my supervisor slowly...a little at a time. When I saw that the person over me was ready to explode, I would apologize profusely. They would see me acquiesce...and humble myself before them...and all was forgiven.

Because I did that so often and they fell for it so often, I thought I was really powerful. That is what gave me the adrenaline rush. Just the thought that I was more intelligent, and skillful than my supervisors...made me feel powerful.

When I did this...I was in control of my life...not my supervisors, or the Navy.

My PTSD was created, because of the fear I felt during the firefight. I felt like I was so vulnerable, that I could possibly be killed.

I never wanted to feel that compromised again, so fighting back against a perceived enemy (my supervisors) made me feel like I was in control. When I disobeyed them, I was not afraid...and I got the adrenaline rush I craved.

When I said that I was in control of my life, during my last few years in the Navy and not my supervisors...that was not entirely correct. I really believed it at the time, but in the last few years, I have realized what was really going on.

All these years, I thought that I was the superior one in those verbal battles. In hindsight, decades later, I realized that I was not the superior one, I was the damaged one.

The reason my superiors let me get away with being so belligerent to them...was that the officers, who I rarely came in contact with, knew by my attitudes and behaviors that the Vietnam war ruined me.

I told you that my lack of emotions...such as, sympathy, empathy, happiness and love...are major symptoms of my PTSD. I thought...that not having these emotions was a normal part of my personality. Even though my lack of emotions was keeping me from having positive relationships, I thought...there was nothing I could do about it, because that was who I was. I have recently realized that my lack of positive and negative emotions are not personality traits, but they are a function of my dysfunctional PTSD brain. That means that this unemotional person that I have been for the last 49 years is not who I am, but it is who my brain is telling me that I am.

Anyone who has been around me for more than 10 minutes can tell you that showing my emotions...or talking about my emotions...is a very rare thing for me to do. In fact, the last time I remember crying in private...or in public...was when I was 19 years old.

The reason that I suppressed my emotions was to avoid distressing memories and thoughts. My PTSD event in Vietnam was so traumatic for me that I did not want to remember how I felt during at that time. I remember to this day distinctly what happened, but I have to dig deep to remember how I felt.

Since I have been making podcasts...and I have unlocked the 'fight-or-flight' mode in the Amygdala part of my brain...I have not only been able to feel some emotions that I have not felt for 50 years...but I have also been able to recall exactly how I felt during the firefight that caused my PTSD.

I can remember distinctly the events of the firefight, and I also remember how scared I was. But, I don't remember how I felt.

A few days ago, as I was talking to a friend about my PTSD. As we were talking, a vision came into my mind.

I was looking down at the firefight I had been in. For a moment, I felt the same way that I had felt during the firefight. It was very scary. That was the first time that I had felt anything about the firefight. Before this...the firefight had just been a memory.

So, why did my brain lock me up in the fight-or-flight mode? It was because, my brain did not want me to feel that kind of pain again. My brain thought it was doing me a favor. In reality...locking up my emotions created a dysfunctional life for me, that not only eliminated the negative emotions, but the positive ones also.

I don't know all the damage my brain did to me over the next few years, but this is what I can piece together.

During that firefight, I believed that emotions could get me killed. And...they could have. So, my brain locked in on not showing or feeling any emotions in a combat situation. Well, after Vietnam, there weren't any more combat situations.

So, to justify keeping my brain in the fight-or-flight mode, my brain had to think I was going to be in more combat situations. So, in effect, because my brain wanted me to be in combat situations, it created them.

When someone would disagree with me on any topic, and I started to argue with them, my brain perceived this to be a combative situation. Not a combat situation, but combative. So, my brain would automatically switch to the fight-or-flight mode to help me win the argument. It worked for me and it worked for my brain.

I liked being in the fight mode, because it helped me win arguments. My brain was reinforced by a positive outcome, so it was validated for putting me in the fight-or-flight mode. So, from then on, my brain began to perceive that every combative situation...as a real combat situation.

In reality, those arguments were combative situations...but they were not equal in intensity, like a real combat situation. They were more like an average argument, disagreement, accident, or any other situation that could cause me to feel similar to what the firefight was like.

So, with the combination of my desire to have another adrenaline rush and my brains effort to push down my emotions, I was a terror when it came to arguing with someone. I purposefully ramped up the hostility in my voice, I put myself in attack-mode...then I fought for my point of view, until I had either won the argument, or conceded.

I know that I am out of the fight-or-flight mode now...because of what happened a few nights ago.

I woke up in the middle of the night. I followed my usual routine when I get up. I turned on the TV to a relaxing music station and picked up the book that I was reading. When my mind has sufficiently relaxed...and I was not in the fight-or-flight mode...I had this revelation about one of the symptoms of my PTSD. I wondered why I didn't feel any emotions. This is what came to me:

The only way to not be crushed by the pain, is to feel no pain, nor sadness, nor depression, nor happiness, nor joy. No pain is all that matters. It is a matter of survival, not just living.

Life without happiness may be bland, but life with pain is unbearable. Even though I realize that this is a sad way to live, it is the only way I can live.

Then I wondered, 'why do I feel that way, and with so much passion and resolve'? Someday, I will know the answer to that question. Not now, but someday.

Then I realized that I am constipated...emotionally constipated. That is the answer. I am all stopped up emotionally.

They tell me that someday, all this emotion what I have backlogged will all of a sudden, just flow out.

Then I wondered...what would make it start to flow? And why would I let that happen?

I wonder if that will ever happen to me? I don't think...I will ever let it happen. I really don't see how it could ever happen. I wonder why that is?

Then I went back to bed.

In the morning, I read what I had written in the middle of the night.

In the past, when my normal way of thinking, was in the fight-or-flight mode, I would have thought those were good ideas, but they really didn't apply to me. Those were just good ideas for other people, but not me.

The reason I thought like that was because I was in my fight-or-flight mode. When I am in that mode, my brain cannot process those kinds of emotional ideas about myself. In the fight-or-flight mode there is no place to process those kinds of thoughts.

Those kinds of thoughts have to be stored in the emotionally active part of the brain, and in the fight-or-flight mode, that part of my brain is in lock-down.

So, when I was relaxed and my fight-or-flight mode was unlocked and my brain returned to the normal mode, I could think those emotional types of thoughts. But, when my brain went back to what was the normal fight-or-flight mode for me, those thoughts were erased from my mind.

But it was different in the morning. Not only could I still remember having those thoughts...but I could still understand why I felt that way.

That is how I know that my brain is now out of the fight-or-flight mode, and permanently in the normal mode.

Now...does that mean that I am fixed? No, it doesn't. It means that even though my brain is functioning in the normal mode, I still have to deal with all the bad attitudes and habits that I developed while I was in the hostile and defensive fight-or-flight mode.

Even though my brain is thinking in the normal mode...I still need someone to tell me what those bad attitudes and habits are...because I have used those bad attitudes and habits to defend myself for so long that I think they are normal...which they aren't. They have been destructive to me for the last 50 years and they are still going to be destructive, until I consciously change them.

The traumatic events that solidified my PTSD over the next two years in the Navy...after Vietnam.

Our KSB unit had only been on our floating dock for about a month...when all of a sudden there were explosions in the small village of Chau Doc that was on the riverbanks about 100 feet from us.

We all quickly gathered on the side of our floating dock. A few of the Vietnamese soldiers were with us. We asked them what was going on...because we didn't have a clue...and we were a little concerned.

They told us that the Viet Cong were firing mortar

shells into the center of the village. After a few explosions...we were very concerned about our safety...so, we asked them if we were in any danger. They told us that we were not, because the Viet Cong did not fire on Americans.

Since we didn't have anything to worry about...we watched the rest of the barrage like it was a 4th of July fireworks display.

This was another traumatic event where I felt like my life was being threatened.

My next traumatic event was when I saw my first dead American.

Every time a helicopter landed on our flight deck...an alarm would sound loud enough for the whole boat to hear. When that happened about 10 of us were assigned to go up on the flight deck and stay there until the helicopter had safely landed.

That was called a fire-watch.

We were there in case a helicopter crash-landed. I didn't know what I was supposed to do if that happened, but I went there whenever I was on the rotating schedule.

Late one evening, a helicopter was coming and the alarm went off. It was my turn to be on the flight-deck, so I made my way up there.

After the helicopter had landed...a dead body...in a

black body bag...was unloaded and transported on a gurney to the boats doctor's office. The doctor's office was only a few feet from my station on the flight deck, so I hung around to see what would happen next.

The door to the office was open, so I walked over to it and stood outside. The body bag was laid out on a table. I saw the doctor and his assistant unzip the body bag. There was a blond-haired 20-year-old Marine laying in the body bag on the table.

It was very unnerving. He didn't look like a combat soldier; he looked more like a surfer catching a wave on Mission Beach in California.

It was very unsettling, but I really didn't know what to do...so I just went back to work.

I was in my first firefight that I told you about...shortly after that happened. A few weeks after my first firefight, I went out on another night patrol with the South Vietnamese soldiers on the Ving Te canal.

This time, the South Vietnamese soldiers I was with set up an ambush on the side of a mountain. We docked our boats...and started to climb up the side of the mountain.

We climbed until we came to a ridge that overlooked a valley. We were told that North Vietnamese soldiers had infiltrated the valley...and had set up several camps in that area.

The South Vietnamese soldiers I was with...set up our camp on a ledge overlooking the valley. As we were standing above the valley on the ridge, we could see the enemy's camp down below us.

Another unit of South Vietnamese soldiers had gone into the valley to clean out the camps.

After it got dark, the fighting started down below us. Because it was dark, we couldn't see any of the soldiers on either side. But, we could see tracer bullets from the South Vietnamese soldiers M-16's and the North Vietnamese soldiers AK-47...flying everywhere below us.

The M-16's the South Vietnamese soldiers were firing...shot a red tracer bullet every 4th round. The tracer bullets created a red line, so they could see where the bullets were going.

All of a sudden...I was back in combat again...and this time...instead of being scared stiff...like the last time...this battle was exciting to me.

That was because...as I watched the red lines going in every direction...the adrenaline started pumping through my body...just like it did in the previous firefight...and this time...instead of being scared spitless...the adrenaline rush felt good.

This time...instead of being paralyzed by the thought of being killed...I wanted to get closer to the battle. The thought of feeling bullets flying over my head wasn't scary at all...in fact...it was exhilarating.

So, what do you think my brain told me to do...so I could get a higher adrenaline rush? It told me to go down into the valley so I could get closer to fighting.

At that moment...I was standing next to the Vietnamese soldier in charge of our unit.

I turned to him and told him that I was going to go down in the valley and take a closer look at the battle that was going on.

Of course, he told me not to go anywhere, but to stay put. I argued with him for a few minutes...until I regained my senses and realized that he was right. So, I shut up and watched the bullets flying...wondering if anyone was getting killed.

Later...when the adrenaline subsided...I realized that going down into that valley...would have been a very dangerous...and stupid thing to do.

Soldiers were getting killed down there...and if I had gone anywhere near the shooting...I could have been wounded, captured, or even killed.

At the time, I didn't know that the strategy the North Vietnamese used in combat was different than our fighting strategy. They did not line up against their enemy, or stay in groups, when they attacked, like we did.

Their soldiers spread out and surrounded their enemy, so they could attack them from all sides.

They hid behind trees and bushes and wait quietly

until you are right next to them. Then they shoot you...and usually you never saw them.

Sometimes, if you are lucky enough to catch them moving, and you could sneak up on them.

Sometimes, when you came face to face with one of their soldiers in the jungle...the one left standing was the one who pulled the trigger first.

I didn't know about any of this when I told the South Vietnamese captain, that I wanted to get closer to the battle going on. Logic had left my brain, and the only thing I wanted was to get more of an adrenaline rush. And to do that I had to get closer to the action.

There were a few other firefights, and mortar barrages, that I was involved in after this. I have not talked about them to anyone over the years...because they were not as scary as my first firefight on the canal...and they really didn't make for good stories.

As more of our 50 boats went out on patrol every night...more of them started breaking down. In order to keep them on the canal, we had to work longer hours and more days. More hours meant 12-hour days, and more days meant 7 days a week. It was the middle of January by now.

As a result, my body became so fatigued...from working 12 hours a day, 7 days a week...that I came down with a cold. It was a normal cold at first. I had a low fever, but no other symptoms. I kept working my normal hours.

As my cold go worse, and a fever set in. The fever drained my energy...and I got very fatigued. I got so worn out...that I started taking short naps during our lunch breaks.

After about 2 weeks of this, I developed a very high fever. I had been complaining to my supervisor for a few weeks about this. I told him I was really sick...and I needed to see a doctor.

He said I wasn't that sick...and for me to get back to work. The more I complained, the madder he got. He told me that I could not take a day off, even if I was sick.

I told him that I wouldn't work any longer and that I had to see a doctor. He finally gave in. But, there wasn't a doctor within 50 miles...so, he sent me to a military dentist who was on a boat like ours...about 10 miles up the river.

When I got to the dentist's office, he did a quick examination...and told me that I was not sick enough to be off work. He said he would not sign anything to relieve me from my duties. Then, he sent me back to my unit.

After that, I did not get any better...in fact...I got worse. A few weeks later, I had developed a much higher fever. When I looked like I was going to collapse at my work bench...they finally sent me to a military medical clinic on an Army base...down the river about 50 miles. This was in February.

In the clinic, I finally saw a real doctor. He was disgusted that I was so sick and hadn't received any treatment yet. He diagnosed me with double pneumonia.

That means I had pneumonia in both lungs. He prescribed bed rest for 6 weeks...with a penicillin shot every 6 hours for 2 weeks.

I was pretty much delirious by the time I got back to my boat, so I hit my rack and stayed there for a week.

Once, I had recovered enough to get out of bed...I just had to rub it in. So, I went down to the barge where my unit was working...and sat down next to them...and watched them work for a couple of hours. What made it even better was that my supervisors were close by and I totally ignored them.

That is when my attitude made a dramatic change. I went from wanting to be a good sailor...obey orders...and respect my superiors...to trying to be the worst sailor in the Navy.

Now I realized that my supervisors really weren't concerned about me...or my co-workers. Not only were they not concerned about us...but we were an irritant to them.

It seemed to me that they were treating us like kids, it was okay to be seen, but not heard. Looking back at the military from a better vantage point, I realize that that is actually the way the military operates. It is a class system, where everyone knows their place, accepts it, and obeys the unwritten rules.

My problem was that I didn't understand it...and I didn't want to understand it. So, because I didn't want to go along with it, I decided to fight it.

And that is what I did, not only for the rest of the time I was in Vietnam, but for the next 2 ½ years that I was in the Navy.

By this time, I felt like I was not only being misused by my superiors...but that I was being abused. Like I said, I felt way because I didn't understand how the military operated.

Here's a side note to my story. I had been raised in a Christian religion. I was taught that we were supposed to strive to be as perfect as we can be. The way to become perfect is to learn to love everyone. To achieve this goal, we all cooperate and try to help each other become better people.

I didn't see that where I was stationed in Vietnam. In fact, I saw just the opposite. I saw leaders trying to intimidate and belittle their subordinates.

This seemed upside down to me. I tried to reason with my supervisors and help them understand what I expected from them. Of course, because that is not the way the military operated, they just laughed at me. Then they made fun of me.

They told me over and over again...that I was either with them or against them.

In a war zone, you are encouraged to lock up your emotions, because in order to kill another person, you can't have any feelings about them. You can't kill someone you love, but you can kill someone you hate.

In this hostile, angry, and chaotic environment, I couldn't love my supervisors. They didn't deserve it. I couldn't even just become apathetic...and accept what they were doing to me.

It seemed to me that I was in a jungle environment, where the law of the jungle rules. That is that the biggest and baddest survive by beating down everyone else. When you do that, they leave you alone. That is the way to survive in the jungle. Make the big bad guys afraid of you, so they will leave you alone.

I felt like I was getting eaten alive by beasts that were bigger and badder than I was. So, in order to survive in this jungle, I had to be bigger and badder than my competition.

In my mind, my competition were my supervisors. I decided that the way to beat them, was to make them afraid of me. The way to that was to stand up to them.

When I made that decision, after my bout with the pneumonia, I had no idea that I would be going against the whole culture of the military.

So, how do I go about doing that.

The first thing I did was set some rules of engagement...or...guidelines for myself.

#1 – I did not want my attitudes and behaviors to be so objectionable that my supervisors would have a reason to put me in the brig or kick me out of the Navy.

#2 – I didn't want to hurt anyone; I just wanted them to leave me alone.

#3 – I still had to live with my fellow sailors, so I didn't want to offend everyone or make everyone hate at me.

So, how was I going to do that?

I decided that verbal battles with my supervisors would be easy to win. Nothing physical, just a lot of talk. I had learned to be a public speaker in my church, so that seemed to be an easy thing for me to do.

Then, if I was going to be the biggest and baddest verbal beast in the jungle, I would have to add a lot of emotion to my discussions. I would have to learn to be rebellious and disobedient, with class.

I couldn't be so rebellious and disobedient that I got put in the brig or kicked out of the Navy, but I had to make them really mad at me without motivating them to take any disciplinary action.

I succeeded in doing just that. I talked back to my supervisors and I disobeyed orders. But I always had a logical reason for what I was doing or saying that made some sense to them, and with so much emotion that they did not know how to handle me.

My mantra became, 'Yea, though I walk through the valley of the shadow of darkness, I will fear no evil...for I am the baddest beast in the valley'.

I thought that my strategy was brilliant. But in hindsight, I can see that my supervisors just felt sorry so me because I was so broken from my Vietnam experience, that they just left me alone, and told my co-workers to do the same.

This was in February.

Then the firefight that caused my PTSD happened in March.

In my research of PTSD, I have learned that whatever attitudes, personality traits, and behaviors you have when a traumatic event happens and you develop PTSD as a result of that traumatic event, that those attitudes become a permanent part of you...no matter how you acted before.

I had been a submissive, obedient sailor before I went to Vietnam. After the firefight, my negative attitude towards the military that should have lasted only while I as in Vietnam, became permanent.

In other words, my PTSD brain locked up all the

temporary dysfunctional personality traits, attitudes, and behaviors and made them a permanent part of me.

As a result, those negative attitudes and behaviors have been who I am for the last 50 years. Who I was is long gone.

Now, this is what happened to me a few months after my firefight in June.

My hostility towards my supervisors began growing...more every day. Not only were they doing nothing to decrease my hostility...they were adding fuel to the fire.

So...I decided to take the initiative...and see if I could change my desperate situation by myself.

I started talking to my co-workers about how bad our working situation was. They all agreed with me that something needed to change or we would all go crazy.

We decided to talk to our lieutenant to see if he would do something to help us.

Our Lieutenant agreed to meet with the 4 of us. We told him we were very unhappy with our working conditions and we needed his help.

This would be the first time I had actually talked face-to-face with my Lieutenant. I had said 'hi' and 'yes sir' to him, but I had never had a conversation with him.

As the meeting began, he said to us, "I understand

that you think that we are not supporting you. Why would you think that?"

Then...he was quiet and just stared at us. As he stared each of us down...no one said a thing. When no one spoke up, I jumped in. I said, "I think you don't care if we are successful or not. You won't get us the parts we need...and you are working us way too hard".

He began to explain to us why we weren't getting our parts...and then he stopped in mid-sentence. He looked at me...and said, "so, Mills...you think I am not doing my job. Obviously, you don't like working here'"

Then...he was about to say something else to defend himself...but he stopped in mid-sentence. Then he lowered the boon on me. He said, "since you don't like it here, I am going to transfer you to a different unit."

My jaw dropped. I was not expecting anything like that. I told him that he couldn't do that, because no one had ever been transferred out of our unit.

He told me that he just did it...and that the meeting was over. Then he stood up and walked out of the room.

The other guys just looked at me and one of them said, "boy you are in deep doo doo".

Regardless of what I thought happened in that meeting back then...today...in hindsight...I have to say that he was right and I was wrong.

At that time, I had been in the US Navy for a year and a half, I still didn't understand anything about how the military operated.

I actually thought that I had more rights than I did. I had no idea that what I thought...or wanted...had little to do with what I got from my supervisors.

This was my wakeup call. At that moment...I realized that I was powerless to do anything I wanted...and that the Navy didn't. This made me frustrated, angry, hostile, and a lot of other adjectives.

So, what was I going to do about it? At that time, I really didn't know what I could...do about it.

So, I just let it fester, and kept my hostile thoughts to myself.

The next day I received a letter from the commander of the boat stating that I was being transferred to the Head shop in the mechanic's room.

That is not the marijuana shop. It is where the top section of the diesel engines go to get overhauled. That part of the engine is called the Head...and it sits on top of the cylinder block.

I had to have someone show me where the Head shop was. He led me to the back of the boat into the mechanic's room. There was a guy standing over a work bench assembling a part of a diesel engine. I was introduced to him and told that I would be working here until my year in Vietnam was over.

After spending a few days with him, I was happy about the transfer, because he was a good guy. He was really good at the work he was doing and enjoyed doing it. He said the work was interesting and the training would be good for him. He said he was going to get a job doing that on the outside.

Then he told me that my supervisors couldn't decide what to do with me, so they put me with him...and he was OK with that.

Well...that was not the end of my punishment. In a week or so, a guy came to me and told me that I was being transferred to the Ving Gi Army Base for a 30-day rotation.

I was happy about that because a month before...I had asked to be transferred there. It sounded like a fun place to be and it would get me away from the boat and my unit.

Shortly after getting that news, I was telling another guy about my transfer...and how I was happy about it, so they must not be that mad at me. He laughed and said, they were not sending me there because I wanted to go there...they were sending me there as a punishment.

Then, I got mad all over again.

So, I packed my seabag and, in a few days, I got on a helicopter and headed for the Ving Gi camp. When I got there, I realized that it really was a punishment.

That Army Base was 50 miles from nowhere...and about 10 miles from the Cambodian border. It was manned by about 40 South Vietnamese soldiers and 10 American soldiers. Two of us were sailors.

The only way in or out of the camp was by helicopter. There were no roads in or out.

There were some women there who were civilians, so they must have been the wives of some of the Vietnamese soldiers. They did the cooking and the laundry.

There were 4 howitzers on the base that were firing shells to the west of the camp every 30 minutes, all day long. A howitzer is a short barrel gun that can shoot higher than a cannon, but lower than a mortar.

I don't know what the guns were aiming at, because the shells were landing so far away that I couldn't hear them explode. A howitzer shell can travel up to 19 miles.

The gun fire in the camp was deafening. Today, I am on VA disability for hearing lose because of that.

The base was next to a muddy canal about 30 feet wide. I don't know how deep it was because, no one swam in it. But the women did the camp laundry in it.

Each of us had to pay them to do our laundry. I was so ticked off at being there, that I did not want to pay to have my laundry done...so I went down to the canal to do it myself.

The women kneeling next to the bank doing laundry were laughing at me for trying to get my clothes clean in muddy water. I wasn't having any success, so it was obviously harder than I thought it would be. After 5 minutes, I gave up and paid the women to do it.

The food was good, but there were so many flies all over the camp that when we ate, we had to brush the flies off our plate between every bite. Take a bite, swish the flies, take another bite.

We bunked in Quonset huts. They were about 50 feet long and 20 feet wide. Each one housed about 30 people. Each of us had a mosquito net around our cot. I was glad for that, because the mosquitoes were giant.

The camp was on a flat plain. There were no trees for miles, only prairie grass. Therefore, there was no shade in the camp or anywhere around it. That was good because it was easy to see the enemy coming from a mile out.

The camp was attacked by North Vietnamese soldiers a couple of months earlier. No one in the camp was killed. They killed some of the attackers, before they retreated.

Too add to all that, the temperature during the day was around 115 degrees with about 90% humidity. Because of that, we didn't wear our uniforms, we just wore our fatigue pants and T-shirts.

Once I figured out how bad the living and working conditions were, I was really ticked off. Therefore, my attitude was not very accommodating towards my supervisors. In fact...I was pretty hostile.

I guess my supervisors did not appreciate that. I know that...because one day while we were doing some busy work in the 115-degree heat, I was so hot, sweaty, and tired, that I kind of lost it.

It was blistering hot and our supervisors decided we had to do something besides just sit around the base, so they had us take apart our Quonset hut and move it about 10 feet from where it was.

They wanted us to take apart every piece of the hut, move the wooden deck 10 feet and put it all back together again. One of the Americans started complaining about having to take it all apart.

He said that we didn't have to disassemble every part, all we had to do was detach the frame from the base, move the base, then put the frame back on the deck and we could be done.

That sounded sensible to me, so I suggested that to one of my supervisors. He laughed and said, "no way we are doing that, take every piece apart."

It was hot and we were sweating, so I kept telling him how stupid it was to make us do this. He finally gave up and that is what we did.

Here's the problem. I didn't realize that they were

having us do that because it was just busy work to get us off our duffs and get some exercise. I thought they really wanted to move them.

So, when they gave into my incessant complaining, they were really mad.

I know that because an hour later, one of them came to me and said that I was being sent back to my outfit on the YRBM 20. I told them that I had only been there 3 weeks of my 30-day rotation.

He told me it didn't matter that they were tired of my hostile attitude and I was to pack my seabag, go to the helicopter pad and wait for the helicopter that would be there in 2 hours. There was no shade anywhere around the helicopter pad.

In 2 and a half hours, I was back on the YRBM 20 filing down valves for the diesel engine heads.

I had been tamed by that time, and I was quiet for the last 2 months of my duty in Vietnam. In September, I headed back to the States.

As I sat in the transient barracks in the evening before my flight out, I was thinking about how happy I was to be getting out of Vietnam. Then the thought came to me that I might not wake up in the morning in time to make to the airport for my 6:00 flight back to the states. I got so scared that I would miss my morning flight, that I got on the last bus from the transient barracks to the airport at 10:00 at night.

When I got to the airport waiting area, I realized that there was nowhere to sleep. I also realized that I couldn't go to sleep, because there was no one there to wake me up in the morning for my flight. So, I stayed awake all night walking around the airport to make sure that nothing was going to keep me from going home.

I flew into San Francisco and took a bus to Treasure Island Naval Base nearby. The personnel office there didn't have any orders for me, so they told me to take 30 days leave, then come back there and my orders would be waiting.

After my 30 days at home in Eugene, Oregon, I went back to the Naval Base in San Francisco. They had my new orders this time.

I was transferred to an LPD that was stationed at the Long Beach Naval Station, in Long Beach, California, near Los Angeles.

My first day on the ship, I told my shipmates that I was glad to be there, because I had had some really bad duty stations. They laughed and told me that this ship was going to be worse than anywhere I had been. That surprised me, because the working conditions seemed to be very good.

But, after a few weeks, I found out what they were talking about. The supervisors were very condescending to everyone below them. Communication was poor and the orders they gave were very vague.

They were right about the lousy working conditions on that ship. So, when I realized that, I told them they were right and I was going to get off this ship as soon as I could figure out how to do it.

They laughed again and told me no one ever got off this ship and I would be here for the next year and a half until I was discharged from the Navy.

Of course, that didn't sit well with me, so I started looking for a way to get transferred.

In the meantime, I had to decide how I was going to deal with more incompetent supervisors. Very few sailors in the Navy were shore-duty in Vietnam. I didn't know any other person on the ship that had been stationed in Vietnam. That made me an anomaly, and I played it for everything it worth.

They assigned me to do some work in the ship's engine room. I told them that I had only worked on outboard motors in Vietnam and that I didn't know how to do what they wanted me to do. But...I told them...I could watch the other guys do it...and maybe I could do it myself the next time.

They seemed to be OK with that, so I followed the crew to the engine room and watched them complete the job.

The ship had a maintenance schedule of the things

that needed to be checked and fixed over the whole year. So, we didn't do the same job very often.

Since it worked the first time, I used it every time they asked me to do a new project.

After a few months, they got the idea that I wasn't going to any work for them at all as long as I was on the ship.

That is how I had learned to beat the system...and not get in trouble.

Since not doing anything seemed to be the way to go, and not working was kind of fun, I decided that if I couldn't be the best sailor in the Navy, that I would be the worst.

And that is what I became. I was a mechanic, but for the next year and a half in the Navy, I didn't do any mechanical work. In fact, I did not do anything that even resembled work.

If my superior told me to repair an engine part...I told them I didn't know how to do that particular repair, and therefore, I couldn't be trusted to do it. I told them that if I watched someone else do it one time, I might know how to do it the next time.

Then...when the next assignment rolled around, I used a similar excuse.

I told my supervisors...that I was so incompetent...so many times over the next few months, that they quit asking me to anything on my own.

In private...with my co-workers, I questioned everything we were told to do.   I didn't say that we shouldn't do it, I just said it was unnecessary...that we do it right now, and that we should do it later.

I was very effective in getting my co-workers to work slower than our supervisors wanted us to.

I also became very good at causing hate and discontent among my shipmates. Since they had complained to me about how bad the ship was, I made it my daily goal to point out to them all the things that were wrong with our supervisors, the ship, and the Navy.

I started leaving the work parties I was assigned to...and went somewhere in the ship that I wasn't supposed to be. I would show back up...when I thought the job would be over.

I was so successful at doing this, that it became a habit, then a daily occurrence. My supervisors seemed to tolerate it, so I kept it up.

At the time, I thought that I was the smartest person in the room and that is why they let me get away with being so disobedient.

In hindsight, I realized years later, that they didn't

think I was the smartest guy in the room at all, they could see that Vietnam had broken me. Because they didn't know how to fix me, and didn't know what else to do with me, they just let me incoherently ramble around the ship.

I was on the ship about four months when they announced that we were going to leave for a six-month cruise around the Pacific Ocean. It was actually a scheduled West Pacific Ocean assignment.

We were to go to the Philippines and pick up some supplies, take them to DaNang Vietnam, go to Singapore, pick up some supplies and take them back to the Philippines. We were to do that for six-months.

After a month of doing that, I had to get off that ship. Mostly because I didn't like it, but mainly because I had told the guys that I could do it.

One day, a brilliant idea hit me. I could volunteer to go back to Vietnam. Because I had been there once, they would surely send me back. That was my way off the ship.

So, I immediately went up to the personnel office and told them that I wanted to volunteer to go to Vietnam. They looked at me like I was crazy, but they said they would submit my request.

A month later, I got new orders to report to an LST in the Mekong Delta region of Vietnam. I was elated that I had accomplished my goal of getting off the ship.

Then one evening as I was walking off the ship to go downtown, I walked by the TV room off the mess hall and the 6:00 news was on the TV. They were reporting on what was going on in Vietnam. It showed a group of South Vietnamese soldiers racing up a hill to engage the enemy.

As I watched it, all of a sudden, the fear, anxiety, frustration and all of the other negative feelings rushed through my body. When that happened, I realized that I did not want to go back there. It was a bad place to be. I had hated it when I was there and I would hate it when I was there again.

I realized that I had blocked out all of those negative, disastrous feeling when I left Vietnam. Until now!

But...I already had orders to go back, so I blocked out all those negative feeling...again.

As I reflected on how I felt as I watched that news reel clip, I remembered that I really did hate being in Vietnam. In fact, I hated everything about it. But now I was going back there.

Oh well, there was nothing I could do about it now. Maybe the second time wouldn't be as bad.

As my departure time started getting closer, I went

up to personnel office and asked them what part of Vietnam I was going to.

They said I was to catch the LST somewhere in Vietnam, but they didn't know where exactly. They looked at my orders again and told me that the orders said I was to report to the Naval Base in Guam. I asked why, and they said they didn't know, that is just what my orders stipulated. I was supposed to fly out of Singapore to Guam.

So, in a few weeks, I packed up my gear, headed to the airport and flew to Guam. When I arrived in Guam, I went to the base personnel office and asked them where my boat was in Vietnam.

To my utter surprise, they told me the LST wasn't in Vietnam, but it was headed back to the United States to be decommissioned.

Now that was good news. Not only did I get off the ship...that no one could get off of...but I was not going to Vietnam again...and now I was going home.

The personnel officer did not know where the LST was going in the States. So, he told me to go home for 30 days, then go to Treasure Island Naval Base and they would know where the LST was going to be.

So, I had a great time at home while by shipmates were steaming around in the Pacific Ocean.

When my 30 days was up, I went to Treasure Island again and they told me to report to the Kitsap Naval Base in Bremerton, Washington where the LST was going to be decommissioned. When I got there, they told me that the decommissioning process would be finished in 3 months.

That was more great news, because Bremerton, Washington was only 4 ½ hours from my home in Eugene, Oregon. That would mean I could drive home on weekends.

My euphoria quickly ended as I got out of the taxi and went up the gang plank of the LST. Now, I was back in the Navy again and my PTSD returned with renewed vigor. I was...again...one hostile sailor.

The PTSD that I had developed in Vietnam was in full command of my attitude and behaviors again...and I was angry, frustrated, hyper-active.

However, by this time in my Navy career...I had learned to keep my hostile attitudes to myself, so I wouldn't get punished by incompetent supervisors.

It didn't take me long to find a few sailors that I was working with that had the same feelings about the Navy and Navy leadership that I did. Every day, we commiserated about how bad we were being treated, as we chipped the paint off of the engine room equipment and the bulkheads.

We spent most of the day thinking up ways to get back at our supervisors for being mean to us. We finally came up with a very creative way to "stick it to the man."

Our plan was to take a bed sheet and write on it in red paint, 'the Navy sucks' and hang it just above the gangplank during the night, so everyone would see it when they came to work in the morning.

I get some credit for helping to create the plan but didn't get a chance to help execute it. I was off base the night they did it. When I came to work in the morning, there it was...flapping in the breeze, bold and daring.

The officers on the ship, didn't find out who did it, so no one was punished.

When the crew had chipped all the paint off the boat and painted everything with red lead paint, our job was done.

The next duty station I was assigned to was in San Diego, California. I was to report to the Coronado Amphibious Base and be stationed on board and LCU.

An LCU is a Landing Craft Utility boat. It is used by amphibious forces to transport equipment and troops from ships anchored offshore and land them on the beach.

There was a 7-man crew on the boat. We lived on the boat. We slept and ate there.

I had been in the LCU unit for a few months, when a

guy from the personnel office called me in. He said that he was issuing orders for me to go with the crew of the LCU boat I was on to Okinawa for a six-month tour of duty.

Going to Okinawa wasn't bad, but the timing was hideous. This happened in February of 1972. I was supposed to go to Okinawa in March and stay there until September.

I was due to be discharged from the Navy in June on an early release college program. My enlistment was actually up in October, but the military gave soldiers who wanted to go to college a 3-month early release.

So, I was planning to get out of the Navy in July and now I wasn't going to get out until we got back from Okinawa in September. This was disastrous for me.

I already hated the Navy for what they put me through, and now I even hated them more for what they were going to do to me.

I tried to do what I did best and talk my way out of the transfer by telling the personnel guy all the reasons I couldn't accept the transfer. He said he didn't care about any of my excuses. Of the 4 crewmen on the LCU, I was the only one who was single and didn't have a family or was going to be discharged in a few months. I was his only choice, so he told me to suck it up and live with it.

This was another traumatic event that compounded

my PTSD.

Okinawa wasn't bad but being in the Navy was still a terrible place to be. To make sure my superiors new how much I disliked them, I disobeyed almost every order I was given for the first 4 months I was on the LCU crew.

Then, with only a few months left in my service career, the 1st Class supervisor that was over me called me into his office. He told me that I only had 1 more quarter for him to evaluate me on my performance before I was discharged. He said that if he gave me the quarterly marks that I deserved, I would not get an honorable discharge from the Navy, but I would get a General Discharge.

If I got that type of discharge, I would not get any of the military benefits such as the GI Bill for college, or Veteran home loans. This was the first time I had been rattled since Vietnam. I wanted those benefits.

So, what could I do? I thought about it for a few minutes, then I told him I would make him a deal. In return for him giving me acceptable quarterly marks on my final evaluation, I would obey most of the orders he gave me of the next 2 months.

Since, I had been a total pain-in-the neck since I arrived on the boat, he agreed.

So, from that day on, I set out to be a good sailor, for the first time in years.

September finally came and we were sent back to Coronado Naval Base in San Diego, where I was going to be discharged from the Navy in a week or so.

That day finally came and I was ecstatic. I would finally be a free man. I packed my seabag for the last time with all my personal items and headed for the personnel office to sign out.

I sat fidgeting in my chair while I signed all the discharge papers and there was a stack of them. Finally, the personnel officer said, 'we only have one paper left. All I have to do is add up your quarterly marks'.

There were about 4 pages of quarterly marks, that started when I was in boot camp and went up to my final evaluation a month or so before my discharge date.

About halfway through, he said, 'Oh no' and had a worried look on his face. I asked him what was wrong and he said, 'I don't think your quarterly marks are high enough to get you an honorable discharge'.

Now, instead of being excited about getting out of the Navy, I was mad all over again. I had just been stabbed in the back by another superior who said he would work with me.

The First Class who filled out my final quarterly marks had not done what he said he would do. I did what I told him I would do. I obeyed most of the orders I was given for the last two-months under his command.

But, he had not done what he agreed to do. He had given me low quarterly marks. I was so mad that I told the personnel officer to give me any score that he wanted to. I didn't care if I got an Honorable Discharge or not. I just wanted to get out of this place forever and go home.

He kept adding and when he was finished with the last column, he gave a sigh of relieve and said, 'your score is just above the minimum for an Honorable Discharge'.

I was not relieved; I was still very mad. He filled out the last few forms, stamped them, put them in a manila envelope and handed them to me. I put the envelope in my seabag and stomped out of his office. I walked to the bus stop near the entrance of the base, flopped down on the bench and waited for the bus to come.

The LCU boat was just 100 feet from the bus stop and I couldn't stand to look at it. I had been betrayed again.

I wrote this in 2011, when I was 62.

I do not know all the ways I am different, abnormal, or off the chart wacko. I am in therapy for the 3rd time now. I am seeing a psychologist for PTSD. We are working on understanding why I do not now and never have had any close friends. I am beginning to understand that I see other men as tools to be used for my purposes. Because I am emotionally inhibited, I do not connect except in a task situation. My therapist told me this is not conducive to a real friendship. Who would have guessed? I have always thought that is what friends are for. What else would they be good for?

I am learning not to feel guilty, angry or to blame Heavenly Father for my dysfunctions. I am what I am, good or bad. I have done what I have done, good or bad.

When I applied for PTSD in 1998 based on my experiences in Vietnam, a Psychologist at the Veterans Hospital told me that I did not have PTSD, I had ADHD. I thought about it for about 10 seconds and dismissed it. Since then, I have realized that I do have some of the symptoms of ADHD.

I suffered severe brain damage in the accident I had when I was 8 years old. I can see now that most of the brain damage I suffered had to do with the parts of the brain that control social cues, interpersonal and group relationships. I have always had difficulty understanding what to do in those situations. I have always thought that the trouble I was having was because I didn't know the rules of social behavior, but now I can see that it is because my brain doesn't process the rules. I should know what to do in social situations, but my brain doesn't process what I need to know when I need to know it.

When working with mentally retarded kids, we call that a disconnect in the brain. When the neurons in the brain synapse or send off an electrical charge that is part of a synapse circuit, it is supposed to connect with the next neuron in the circuit. When part of the brain is damaged, that connection isn't there. The neuron in the brain fires, but the next neuron doesn't pick up the signal. It takes many neurons to make a complete a circuit so that the right thing happens in the brain. I have found that that is the case in my brain. Some parts just don't work.

One of the symptoms of the ADHD that I have is that my brain goes either 100 mph or I am at a dead stop, there is no middle ground. The moderator in my brain is broken. That is a result of the brain damage. Add to that the fact that I look at every situation as a battle that I either have to win or walk away from and you can see why I have trouble with interpersonal relationships.

There are lots of examples where I made people mad because I would not let go of something I wanted to make happen, or people I offended because I just had to point out a problem, I saw that they were having, or comments I made in church that nothing to do with the topic, but I just had to say it. The main reason I offend people is because I feel like I have to fix every problem I see.

My therapist pointed out something startling to me. He said that if the other person does not see the problem that I see, the problem doesn't exist. That is amazing to me. All my life I have tried to fix problems that other people do not see. I have never realized that when I try to fix a problem that the other person does not see, that actually makes ME the problem.

I thought these were personality traits. That is just the way I am. But, after 9 months of therapy and discussing what I learn with Peggy, who actually wants me to be normal, I can see that they are not traits that I need to have. The brain damage is minimal at this point in my life. My brain actually started working again when I was 16. I can remember how suddenly things started making sense to me. The problem was that I had learned very little for 8 years old to 16. So, I was way behind the learning curve, especially in social situations.

I was competitive as a child. Then, when I went to Vietnam, I became much more aggressive in my competitiveness. Because winning or losing could be a matter of life or death, I took the competition to a much higher level to make sure I didn't lose. When I came home, I didn't go back to normal. I maintained the same high level of intense competition. I could say my motto was "win or lose but take no prisoners". That is the attitude I have had since then.

This is the reason I shut off my emotions. I can still remember many times between the time I was 8 years old and about 12 that I would lie in my bed at night and get the overpowering feeling that I was all alone in this world. I was living with my parents and siblings, but I still felt like I was completely alone in the house. As I thought about being alone, my whole body would start to ache all over for 15 minutes to half an hour. It was like I was being smothered in a blanket of darkness.

Nothing I could do would make that feeling go away. I would say to myself, 'the only way this feeling is going to go away is if I go to sleep'. After a while I would finally drift off to sleep. It was during that time that I realize now that I decided to block that kind of pain in my life. In fact, I set up defense mechanisms to block all pain from then on.

My life got worse from then on. More bad things happened to me until I decided that the only way I could cope with misery was to shut down my emotions. So, I decided not to feel anything emotionally. I knew how I should feel in emotional situations, but I would not let myself feel anything. I could understand the situation; I would just not feel anything. I would try to understand how the other person was feeling so I could empathize with them. But I would not feel or show any emotion. This began to work for me, so I made it a permanent part of the person I was becoming.

When I was in Vietnam, this attitude was cemented into me. Life was so miserable over there and I was so miserable that it was easier to feel nothing, than it was to feel and cope with all those negative emotions. I learned fast that feelings and showing emotions could get a person killed. If you are going to kill a person, you cannot have any feelings for them or you can't point a gun at them and pull the trigger. If they have a gun pointed at you, you had better be the first one to pull the trigger.

That became my lifestyle and it has been until I married Peggy. Based on a series of things, I realized that burying my emotions was no longer necessary. I was not in Vietnam any longer. The reason I built the defense mechanism to protect myself from negative emotions in the first place, no longer existed. Now I am feeling free to feel. Over the past few years, I have little by little been tearing down those walls I have spent years building for my protection. I am not yet a feeling person, but I am opening myself up to becoming one.

Dave Mills was born and raised in the United States and has lived here all his life. He is 73 years old and a retired public-school teacher. He has taught students with severe disabilities for 20 years. Before that, he was a salesman for about 20 years.

He was taught that America was the land of the free and that it was his duty as a citizen to help keep it that way.

It was his feelings of patriotism towards his country, his duty to defend his country and his desire to protect his family and friends that motivated him to volunteer to join the United States Navy.

He joined the Navy in 1968, when he was 19 years old. At that time, the Vietnam War was in full swing.

6

GOD WILLED IT
Dommartini Salien Sr.

Zero five hundred hours. Wednesday September 10, 2003. Baghdad, Iraq. I'm standing in formation, dress right dressed in my PT shirt and shorts, ready to get the squad leader's accountability report to our platoon sergeant, our platoon sergeant's report to the company commander, and the commander's report to the battalion leader over and done with. I was heading out on my fourth log pack convoy mission today since the day I arrived here.

I was excited inside. Not for that reason though. Oddly enough, the cool dust filled wind I had grown accustomed to was not blowing this morning. Neither were there any Iraqi local nationals anywhere in the motor pool. *I wonder if they'll have any of those fluffy delicious pancakes and spicy sausage for breakfast in the chow hall this morning.* My stomach responded to that thought in my mind with a loud growl.

"Left-face!" our platoon sergeant shouted.

We began our forward march and was soon jogging in cadence to that good old basic training chant.

> *"I don't know why I left,*
>
> *But I must've done wrong,*
>
> *And it won't be long,*
>
> *till I - till I - till I*
>
> *Get on back home..."*

I didn't mind the seven-mile run this morning. Today was a special day for me. It's the day I was born nineteen years ago.

We got back to our tents an hour and a half later and I rushed to grab my hygiene pack to get first dibs on the showers. Waiting in line for the showers usually meant no more fluffy pancakes left in the chow hall and today was my birthday so NO ONE was going to stand in the way of me and a hearty breakfast. I rushed through my shower and other morning hygiene ritual, put my ACU's (Army Combat Uniforms) and boots on, and jetted out of their straight to the chow hall tent. I could smell the heavenly scent the closer I got.

"Hey private, watch where you're going!" sergeant Jones yelled as I accidentally bumped into him on my way to the chow hall.

"My bad sarge!" I hollered back.

I finally made it in the line and there behind the serving counter was my birthday gift to myself! A mountain of pancakes next to a tray of hot steaming roasted spicy sausage, and a server standing in front of a hot skillet ready to make your eggs however you wanted them. I order my breakfast and wolf it down in a matter of minutes. I was eager to know if I was driving on today's mission or if I was a passenger. I hated being a passenger.

As a truck driver in the U.S. Army, there are two things that got under our skin: 1. someone else driving your assigned truck and 2. A mechanic you don't know working on your truck. After breakfast, I met up with my buddy Pounds and we made our way back to the motor pool to get our marching orders for this mission.

"Where do you think we're heading to today man?" I asked Pounds.

"I honestly don't know bro, I think somewhere near Balad" he responded unsure.

Pounds was the only guy here I confided in. He was much older than me by 11 years so I looked up to him like an older brother. He was a wise brotha from New York and never shied away from speaking his mind. I appreciated that about him.

Wherever it was we were going, I did not want to be a passenger. There's nothing like driving a five ton or Humvee through the streets of Baghdad, bumping, and running into any civilian commuter vehicle who wouldn't get out of our way in the convoy. It was almost like playing Mario Kart or something for me. I never really thought about what fear or horror those people driving must have felt seeing our military driving on their roads and essentially shoving them off their roadways.

Someone's voice alarmed me..."SALIEN...PRIVATE SALIEN!"

"Here!" I exclaimed.

It was sergeant Stevens giving out our marching orders, ROE (rules of engagement), and who was driving and riding passenger.

"You're with PFC Williams and you're riding passenger." he ordered.

Dammit, I thought. Williams was a cool individual, nothing against her, but I dreaded riding passenger. We geared up around thirteen hundred hours and I made sure I had fresh rounds in all of my M-4 magazine. We did our final PMCS (preventative maintenance checks and services) on the trucks and our convoy was underway out the gates of BIAP (Baghdad International Airport).

Pure.... blissful....comfort. Those are the words I can use to describe the field of tall flowers that I was laying in on my back. I looked up at the sky and the clouds were changing colors in a vibrant pattern so vivid and ethereal, there was nothing I could do but stare at it all while trying not to hold my breath. A deep, low humming reached my ears and kept me completely mesmerized at all I was experiencing. I did not want to leave this place of safety. This place of refuge. The colorful clouds were now a dark gloomy grey and I no longer heard the soothing hum. I sat up and looked around at the lush field of flowers that were now wilted, decayed, and the smell of death began to fill my nostrils.

Suddenly, it began to rain. Only, it wasn't water droplets that was falling from the sky. They were as small as droplets, but they seem heavier, more metallic, and very hot. More "droplets" began falling all around me leaving searing, steams wherever they fell. I heard a faint screaming voice in the distance!

I woke up abruptly in my seat to a moving truck that's swerving from left to right, a driver who has completely let go of the steering wheel in a panic stupor yelling at the top of her lungs, and I'm taking enemy fire from the buildings we were passing on our right. As bullets were raining on the side door and panels of the truck, I immediately go into marksman mode. Safe to semi. No time to think. You think, you die. I made visual contact with where some of the bullets were coming from and began returning fire.

This started to prove a difficult task for me because Williams was still panicking and had no control of the vehicle. *Is this how I finally go? Is this the way it ends for me?* I thought as I started shouting at Williams.

"HEY, GRAB THE DAMN WHEEL!" I fumed.

After what seemed like an eternity of rocking left and right while shooting at lord knows who and where and a driver yelling in terror, Williams finally gained control of the truck and we drove pass the kill zone for about three miles. The entire convoy comes to a complete stop off the side of a highway and we all dismount to assess any casualties and take up defense positions. I jumped out of my truck and turned to look at how many rounds actually hit our vehicle and nearly fifteen made contact with the door alone.

"Williams, you good?" I yell.

"Yea" she shouts back shakily.

We mounted back up after determining no casualties and made our way back to base. That night, as I laid in my cot inside my tent looking up at the light from the full moon cascading on the tent roof, I thought about that place with the field of flowers.

I often think about that place to this day.

Dommartini Salien, Sr. (aka Martini). is a first-generation immigrant from the island nation of Haiti. He migrated to U.S. in the late 80's with his parents and younger brother by way of South Florida. Martini completed K-12 in South Florida, and later went on to enlist in the U.S. Army as a logistics specialist in 2003.

After serving ten years in the armed forces, two tours in Iraq, being stationed on two continents, and traveling the world, Martini decided to complete his military career in 2012 and pursue his undergraduate degree while simultaneously working for multiple companies in corporate America.

After completing his degree, Martini received a calling to make a huge career shift by becoming a middle school educator teaching brown and black kids in underserved communities while pursuing his graduate degree in business administration as a means to launch his non-profit organization to give brown and black kids vocational skills if college isn't a route for them.

Martini has been an educator for a total of six years and currently lives in Brooklyn, New York with his wife.

7

A Veteran's Love of His Nation
Gregg Cummings

Sometimes in life, we are disheartened by the lack of love and respect in areas that we know hold our moral understandings intact. Those very areas help us to withstand the battles we face throughout our lives. This testimony is a saddening reality it seems, to all of We The People as a whole. I want to sound off with every fiber of my being the service that I have been trying to do, for all of my adult life, and that is to serve the people of this Nation with everything that I am.

I first recognized a love for my country when I was just 7 years old. I can close my eyes and feel that moment as if it just now happened. You see I have three brothers, one twin, and two older brothers, and we would play war in the woods when we were kids, and one day in the fall, the air was cool and the sun was nice and warm, I made me a fort out of some very tall grass, some sticks, and leaves in the side of a small hill.

It was small but when I crawled in laying on my side, I felt as if the country itself was hugging me, letting me know I would be alright and safe. At 7 years old I never knew yet the concept of God, Country, and Freedom, but at that moment, I can tell you, I certainly understood the feeling of it. Later as time went on and I grew up, things fell into place that made my feelings more understood with more detail and more knowledge.

My mother loved country music and I heard the song "God bless America again" by Loretta Lynne, and I understood every word in that song as it directly related to my newfound attachment to the land in which I lived. The main verse in the song pleaded to God: *"God bless America again, you see all the trouble that she's in, wash her pretty face, wipe her eyes, and then, God bless America- again."*

Being the son of a father who served in WWII, and the Korean War and did two tours in Vietnam with two purple hearts and thirty years of service as an enlisted man, I had an upbringing knowing there was a sacredness to our American Flag, the American anthem, and soldiers in uniform. As life went on I actually had American History class in school, not Social Studies that followed later, but an actual class that taught history not the socialization of America.

I learned about the Declaration of Independence, the Constitution of the United States, and the Bill of Rights. I joined the scouts and learned more. I learned so much more as I grew that I knew when I graduated High School I was going to serve in the military and continue to defend this Nation of ours.

I served in the United States Army as a Paratrooper, Engineer, and Ranger. Served in real-world theaters of operations and combat duty, and then later as a military instructor in three different combat-oriented schools. In the civilian sector after my military service, I couldn't help but continue my service to the people.

I got my Sociology degree and worked as a Family Counselor for a while, then as a Police Officer for five years where I was a DRE, Defensive Tactics Instructor, Firearms Instructor, and Less Lethal Munitions Instructor for the state academy. Finally, leaving the force to work nationwide for all fifty states, training and speaking on how to get the people to be more engaged in their local, state, and federal politics, not to strengthen one party over another but to aid in the understanding of the role We The People must take to continue to defend and protect their authority and our founding documents that clearly gives guidance to the same as Frederick Douglas explained so often.

For decades I have attempted to give so much time and effort to help all that I can from small personal aid to local, state, and national education in history, survival, politics, and service to our fellow man. All focused on our sovereignty as individual citizens through the framework of We The People, as laid out in our founding documents. Believe me when I say that I am not sharing all of this to brag by any means. I just want to let you the reader understand that I do have a life of experiences to be able to have a perspective worth hearing. In fact, I would take that statement one step further by saying a veteran's perspective that seems to be eroding with each generation and being forgotten.

While in Iraq my unit lost a total of Ten of my brothers. Ten caskets came home to America with the United States Flag draped over each of them. Then for each of them after the burial ceremony, a commanding officer of the honor guard walks up to the next of kin and says these words:
"On behalf of the President of the United States, please accept this flag as it is presented on behalf of a grateful nation, and its armed forces, as a token of appreciation for your loved one's honorable, faithful, and dedicated service."

At that very moment, that individual soldier became a part of a lineage, a lineage that runs all the way back to the winter of the red snow at Valley Forge and runs through all the 13 wars and service that millions of Americans, of all race, color, and creeds fought and died for the meaning behind the Declaration of Independence, freedom, equality, Constitution, and Bill of Rights, which our sacred flag represents as a whole. From the Revolutionary War to the Civil War to the war in Afghanistan.

The same stood true for all those warriors, many families were affected by the act of service of their loved one, represented in a triangle-folded flag of the United States of America being handed to them to solidify their entry into this lineage of warriors.
Yet today, our children are not taught anything about these protecting warriors of our nation. Very little is even known today about the true sacrifices given nor even present any respect for those who have given their lives for what we do have that is positive in our nation today. The quote often heard; "Lest we forget", used to be understood throughout our society but today veterans seem to be the only ones understanding the sentiment brought forth by it.

The phrase was first uttered by Rudyard Kipling in 1897 who was inspired by the Holy Bible scripture in Deuteronomy 6 verse 12 which reads:
"Then beware lest thou forget the Lord which brought thee forth out of the land of Egypt."
After the first world war, this phrase was adopted as part of Armistice Day traditions as another way of saying we should not forget those that God has put in the position to defend our country.
In closing, this is truly a battle for myself and other warriors who have seen the atrocities of war, seen the

body parts being sorted and placed in caskets and sent back home only to see the lack of love and respect of the sacrifices given in areas of our nation that holds the last burning embers of what made us free in the first place. As for me and my family, we will *"Continue the Mission"* of our nation's founding documents and keep the "Great American Experiment" as President George Washington called it, alive and well... Out here.

Gregg is a US Army Gulf War Veteran ranger, paratrooper, engineer, small arms, and recipient of 23 medals, the Soldiers Medal being his highest during his military career. In his civilian life, he has been a Family Counselor, Police Officer and worked as a Regional Consultant for Strong America Now before working with Tea Party Patriots as a National State Coordinator Manager.

Gregg is the founder of www.continuethemission.net and the author of "Continue The Mission, a We The People's Handbook" as he continues to write about what he loves, his country.

8

UNKNOWN BATTLEFIELDS
Kevin Eastman

<u>Disclaimer</u>: This piece contains racially charged terms some readers may find offensive. I decided to include them not to offend anyone, but to illustrate the factors that can contribute to the magnitude of the internal battles some service members have to fight every day they wear the uniform.

Over 20 years on active duty in the U.S. Air Force. I enjoyed a wonderful career. In that time, I experienced seven assignments, countless temporary assignments in the United States and overseas. I attended training courses, gotten awards, promotions, attended ceremonies, and worked in several different positions, including stints as a military training (drill) instructor, a training manager, and almost 15 years as a recruiter. Not bad for a young man six months removed from high school in Oakland, California, huh?

In 1988, if someone had told me in my senior year of high school, that as a member of a group of only four in my graduating class to join the Air Force, I would accomplish the things I did, I would have told them they were crazy. Especially, given some of the situations I faced during my career. One particular situation early in career left an impressionable mark, and not in a good way. Thinking back on the situation, I'm amazed I made through my *initial* enlistment!

It's no secret that for the majority of its existence, the Air Force is, and has been predominately Caucasian. I searched and found data dating back to 2006, and over a ten-year span in either direction, the statistic hovered around 70% for that demographic. I can't see it fluctuating much less than that, if I could look back at the exact time frame of my first enlistment.

Coming from the environment I grew up in, I had limited interaction with Caucasian people. There were a small number of them in the schools I attended, but for the most part, I was surrounded by African Americans. That atmosphere was flipped on its ear, the day I arrived in San Antonio, Texas for basic training.

In over the course of about twenty-four hours, I went from being the majority, to a very apparent minority. It was a stark contrast to what I was used to, growing up in Oakland. There were ten African Americans in my basic training group of over 40 people. Naturally, it was a culture shock for me, and the pattern continued into my first assignment.

It also tested my mental quite a bit and laid the groundwork for the mental battles I had to regularly fight. This is because throughout my career, I was given reminders at every level, of something I remember being told growing up, but didn't want to believe: I had to be twice as good, to get half as much. The truly sad reality I was faced with was being forced to constantly prove my worth, even to superiors who were familiar with me.

Don't get me wrong. During my career, I worked with some of the most fantastic people in the world! I had a multitude of wonderful people who were willing to pull me aside when needed and give me the guidance that helped shape my career (and life, for that matter). With those wonderful people, I also encountered a number of people who didn't view me as an asset, but an adversary, and did everything they could to stifle my progress. It may not have always been overt, but their actions spoke volumes in my mind. The following was one of those occurrences that contributed to those internal battles I fought for over twenty years in uniform.

Fresh out of basic training, I was settling in at my first assignment, and in the developmental stage of my on-the-job training. I was excited about learning a new skill, though I wasn't working in what I'd call my "ideal" career field. Nonetheless, it was the career field I had at the time, and in order to progress into something different, I needed to be proficient at the job I had. I was trying to learn as much as I could, until I figured out my next career move.

I learned quickly in my career that everyone in the Air Force has a role to play on the team, in order to get the mission accomplished. The unfortunate part of that equation is, everyone in the Air Force doesn't recognize that fact, and may inadvertently, or perhaps intentionally diminish your role on that team. Nothing showed me this more than one particular incident I personally endured.

I was working on a task, with a senior ranking member as my trainer. As a young airman, I was tuned in to everything this man was throwing at me, because I needed to learn the job. After all, he'd been in the Air Force longer than me. That meant he knew more about the job than me, right? Anyway, on this particular job, we didn't have the exact parts we needed to repair what was broken but needed to return the system to functioning as soon as we could, as it was a vital system.

The senior NCO I was working with recognized we needed to do a temporary fix and get the permanent parts to properly fix it later. He conveyed his plan to me, and said, "Don't worry about it. We'll just 'nigger rig' it."

I was shocked by what I heard but wanted to make sure I heard him correctly. I asked, "We're going to do *what* to it?" certain that once he heard my response, it would trigger him to correct his language, or at least apologize for the use of the slur. Unfortunately, he repeated it, as if it was everyday lingo for him, and the second time, I heard him clearly.

My focus on the task went out the window. I turned to him and said, "Sir, you *do* realize I'm black, right?" He responded with "Yes, I know." I then said, "... and you don't see anything wrong with what you said, or that it might be offensive?" His response to my statement was a dismissive one. I can't recall exactly what he said, but basically it amounted to "Be quiet and finish the job." I finished the temporary fix, but when we got back at the shop, I went to the shop foreman with my concerns about what occurred.

The shop foreman and the guy were the same rank, so there needed to be someone with a higher rank in the equation, in case any action needed to be taken. The guy who was the issue was not involved, right away. I was told to go up the chain of command, but when I did, and explained what happened, and how his actions made me feel, I was brushed off, in no subtle terms. Several of the responses I got said essentially the same thing: "Oh, that's just the way he is."

Apparently, his behavior was known by people in the chain, but to that point, nothing was done to curb it. In my head, it translated to, "We know he does it, but because he's knowledgeable about the job, we tolerate it." I was absolutely livid!

Following that sequence of events, a more than modest degree of hesitance was bored, and would eventually remain over the course of my career. My judgement as far as equal treatment was concerned, became jaded. However, as disheartening as the incident turned out, and the way it was handled when I reported it, it could have dejected me. Miraculously, it did the opposite. Instead of souring me on the Air Force, it lit a fire inside of me that's hard to describe.

At times during my career, several similar scenarios played out, and I didn't feel like everyone in the various chains of command I was assigned to, were not as interested in protecting me as a valued asset for the Air Force, as they were in tolerating bigoted ideals, because the person exhibiting the behavior had "experience," or "knowledge." With the unit I mentioned above, the behavior was covered up locally. However, the Air Force as whole saw things differently.

The social actions office was established to address these issues and many others. It eventually transformed into the "EEO" office, which trains Air Force members on maintaining professional relationships. This certainly helped, but it didn't stop the behavior from occurring. What it did, was drive the behavior underground. It was still there – just harder to detect. During a good portion of my career, there were incidents that were evident to me, but since the person knew how to "act" when confronted, the behavior was difficult to prove, which is why my internal battles had to be fought.

At virtually every stage of my career, there was at least one person who I could just tell wasn't as "excited" about my progress as I was and did almost everything they could legally do to impede further progress. Whether it was being passed me over for prime assignments, getting more responsibility that I'd rightfully earned by virtue of my job performance, subverting the accomplishments I'd made, or whatever it was. The actions were not always caught by everyone, and a lot of times, they may have been intentionally ignored, but as many times as they may have been ignored, they were glaring to me.

I dealt with actions like these all the way up to my decision to submit my retirement paperwork. It was mentally exhausting having to regularly contend with an obstacle I had no part in installing personal bias. Even though there were supposed "safeguards" in place to protect people against things like this, the ever-present possibility of repercussions always sat in the back of my mind. If I said something, even anonymously, once the person was summoned, there were probably only a few instances that would have triggered the action they were answering to.

The examples I've used in this piece were centered on black and white, because those were the easiest to identify. However, these types of actions weren't always so cut and cry. I encountered a few sabotage attempts from African Americans as well, which added another level of frustration. I wasn't looking for special treatment of course, but when it was obvious that someone was trying to stifle, or derail your career, in order to advance their own career, it was tough to swallow.

It was so tempting (and easy) to put the race label on many of the situations, when the other person was of another ethnicity, but when the person looks like you, the label may not stick as well. That's when you must start searching for other sources of the contention, and it significantly contributes to the internal battles you fight. When the chain of command is touted to be impartial in all situations, yet fails to support and protect you when you feel you are wronged, who can you turn to?

Fortunately, I managed to find some wonderful mentors during my career (of all ethnicities) that helped me put these battles, as frustrating as they were, into perspective. I realized that anyone had the potential to be fighting internal battles, and personal bias was one of those battles I had to fight. The thing that gave me comfort was a person's personal bias had little to nothing to do with me. They had to look themselves in the mirror, following their actions.

Some of the battles have never been resolved, and personal bias isn't limited to the Air Force. I've encountered it outside of the Air Force, as well. Fortunately, I now have a few more tools in the toolbox. To make the situation more bearable, I did then, and continue to respond as one of my mentors suggested: "Let your performance speak for itself, and never let the Air Force hand you your career. Decide what you want to do, and go after it, until you don't want it anymore."

That was one of the most powerful pieces of advice I was given. The thought process behind it was, if your performance was exemplary, and you established a reputation of knowing your stuff, the only thing someone else could do to stop you would be to bring personal bias into the picture, and then, it would be loud and clear enough for anyone to see.

What was my contribution to personifying that philosophy? I kept my nose clean and continued to excel at every position I worked in, despite the personal biases, and obstacles I encountered. The way I saw it, if a person had a problem with me, *they* had the problem... not me. I enjoyed who I was, and knew what I could accomplish, if given the opportunity. If the opportunity was not given, and I still wanted it, I found a way to *make* the opportunity. Each time I had someone tell me I couldn't do something, my inner response was "Okay... watch this!"

I have no idea what happened to that senior NCO I worked with, and frankly, it doesn't matter to me. In a weird sense, I guess I'm grateful for his actions, and narrow-minded views, because they actually motivated me. In learning from that single incident, I grew to ascend through the ranks, reaching the senior NCO tier, myself. I earned every one of the stripes I wore and had no problem looking myself in the mirror when I looked back on my career, because I knew what I'd accomplished was done with one of the most important character traits a person can have, at the forefront: integrity.

To showcase a few of these accomplishments: I was selected for leadership positions, despite having higher ranking people on the team with me. I was requested (by name) to fill a highly visible position when the primary position holder was going to be out for an extended period of time. The crowning moment for me, was when the team I was fortunate enough to lead, earned the top spot in the country for their performance.

What I learned from those experiences was somebody else was not going define the direction of my career. I was going to take care of that. The battles were there for me to fight regularly, and no one knew the extent of what was going on in my head, unless I told them. Some of the battles were tougher than others, but I was determined not to let any of them break me. I'll admit... a few of them came close at times, but my will to succeed in my Air Force career was stronger than any personal bias, regardless of who it originated from, or their reasoning for it. Looking back, I made sure I applied the philosophy the Air Force trained me on: "The objective is to achieve the goal, regardless of the obstacles standing between you and the goal."

Kevin is a native of Oakland, California, but currently resides in Riverside County, in Southern California. A skilled speaker and business management consultant with a passion for assisting others in achieving their goals, he thrives on simplicity and logic.

A graduate of Castlemont High School, he retired from active duty in the U.S. Air Force with over 20 years of service, in locations around the world, including San Antonio, Texas, Chicago, Illinois, Belize, South Korea, and Japan.

He served stints as a military training instructor (commonly known as a "drill" instructor), and over a decade as a recruiter at the high school, college, and post-graduate levels.

Kevin earned undergraduate degrees Human Resource Management, and Marketing, from the Community College of the Air Force and Columbia Southern University, respectively, as well as a graduate degree in Business Management, Marketing from Azusa Pacific University. He also holds certifications in Marketing, Professional Selling Skills, and Sales Coaching.

With the release of his debut book, *"Don't Gamble on Life Improvement... Until You Shift the Odds!"* he became a published author.

He is an active member of Alpha Phi Alpha Fraternity, Inc., an avid sports fan, and enjoys cooking, writing, meeting people, listening to music, watching movies, mentoring, traveling, and spending time with family and friends.

9

DEATH IS A RELEASE PAIN IS FOREVER
Sgt. Marvis Cox

The day seemed normal, as usual. Birds were chirping, and people were singing Allah Auk-Bak all over the city. Eeriness filled the atmosphere as the temperature started to increase. It's going to be a hot one today, said one of my fellow soldiers pulling guard with me. We were almost done with our twelve-hour guard shift, and I could only think about taking a shower and getting some rest.

Things happening unexpectedly became routine. Watching the nights turn into days became normal six months into the deployment. Thirty minutes left until our replacement comes, and I see a bunch of kids running towards our guard shack, screaming Mr., Mr. help us! Ally-Baba is trying to kill our family!

Everything was in an uproar, and guns were drawn because we couldn't figure out if this was a trick to attack us. Seven Marines had already died weeks before from a scheme similar to this one, so we had to be extremely cautious and stern. "Get back!" "Don't come any closer!"

I signaled one of the soldiers to call headquarters with everything that was happening. I told the other two soldiers to keep their guns drawn just in case things got crazy and to cover me while I assessed the situation. I was able to calm the kids while carefully observing their body language.

My gut instinct gave me the reassurance something was terribly wrong. One of the older kids had blood on his back and shoulders as if they had been fighting or helping somebody in need. "Please come quick!" "Ally-Baba is killing my family!"

Headquarters sent down a QRF (quick reaction force) team to further investigate the situation. The QRF team searched the kids to ensure nobody had weapons or bombs attached to them. The team leader wanted me to go with them since I had already built a good repour with the kids.

We crossed the bob wire and moved in a wedged formation to the objective. We kept the kids in the middle while gathering intel for this mission. As we approached the building, people started to run away as if they knew bad guys were waiting to attack. The kids started pointing and shouting there, in there!!

A door was hanging off the hinges, and blood was on the wall. Then a man came out with a knife in his hand. The kids screamed Ally-Baba! The team approached him carefully while giving strict orders to drop the knife and get on the ground. We detained the individual as the other team rushed into the building to aid the wounded.

Two soldiers stood the attacker up as the team leader called for the interpreter. I couldn't have blinked my eyes more than five seconds before I saw the attacker try to take the team leader's rifle away from him. I immediately took action and disarmed the attacker with great force. The mission was a success, but I hyper-extended my knee during the process. I was on crutches until my knee healed, but I couldn't perform my job as the lieutenant's driver. I had to make sure and study all the roads and landmarks before heading out on a mission.

The lieutenant was a man of few words, but he knew his job. He was always cool under pressure but had zero tolerance for BS! Even though he had the map in his hand, the lieutenant never made eye contact, just pointed left or right, and he expected the driver to know when to turn or stop just by his hand signals.

I knew how much he trusted me to drive, and it felt like I was letting my guys down due to my injury. That evening, my lieutenant came to my room, asking how

I was doing? I was shocked because this is something that doesn't usually happen. He told me how great of a job I did helping take down the guy who tried to take the QRF team leaders rifle and would soon put me in for an award. He told me that a new driver was needed since I was injured. He wanted to know about a fellow soldier and wondered if he could perform the task? I told him sure, once given a chance. He gave a smirk and said get better soon, I need my driver. Without eye contact, he walked away, and that was it.

The next day, my company was tasked with a critical mission. It involved a dangerous highway where my team and I were last ambushed. I remember watching as everybody left. I told them good luck. I felt so disappointed I wasn't going with them. A few hours later, tragedy struck. I was manning the radio when I heard the news. The lieutenant and my buddy had to be medically evacuated. They hit an IED and were hurt extremely bad.

The lieutenant shattered his left leg and fractured his pelvis, and the new driver lost both legs, with multiple fragments to his face. I was devastated by this information. How could this be? All the while, I couldn't help but think that it could have been me! I still feel responsible for what happened to my buddy. I often wonder if he holds a grudge and truly forgave me for what happened. We keep in touch, and I am careful not to bring up the subject because I don't want to open old wounds and lose a friend.

Marvis F. Cox Sr. was born in Chicago, Illinois in the winter of 1981. He entered into the United States Army Infantry, E5 Sergeant was his final rank. He entered the Army in 2001 and was sent to Iraq to serve in the war of Operation Iraqi Freedom (9/11).

Marvis did 9 years overseas (3 deployments) and was honorable discharged due to service-connected disabilities from the war. Marvis has been happily married for seven years to his wife Jacquiline. They have a blended family of five children of whom he loves deeply.

Marvis graduated College in 2015 with two Associates degrees from Waubonsee College. He is a Life Coach for urban and troubled youth and is also a Motivational Speaker.

Marvis plans to continue to write and give back to his community as much as possible. He hopes to one day open his own nonprofit so troubled youth can come and learn discipline and leadership skills to assist them with becoming successful, despite the difficulties and challenges of their environment.

10

THE OTHER SIDE OF WAR
Mary L. Beal

Philosopher George Santayana said: "Those who cannot remember the past are condemned to repeat it." Condemned in the sense that the horrors of the past are repeated. So, a real sense of history is a good thing and is best developed by an "in context" approach to an event.

Former Secretary of State George C. Marshall stated in a speech in 1947, "I need not tell you, gentlemen, that the world situation is very serious. That must be apparent to all intelligent people. I think one difficulty is that the problem is one of such enormous complexity.

The mass of facts presented to the public by the press (newspaper, magazine, television, internet) and radio make it exceedingly difficult for the man in the street to reach a clear appraisal of the situation."

Seventy years later, this is still true, even more complex with the invention of television and the internet.

The activities of the United States military over the last seventy-five years have been enormous and complex. As a professional managerial civilian employee Department of Defense for almost thirty years, I witnessed, directly and indirectly, some of the complications of military life.

I worked in the continental United States and overseas. I even had an opportunity to experience inside a war zone. Also, as a military family member, I experienced the impact of deployments on the family left behind. I had an older brother who served in the United States Army during the Korean Conflict. My youngest brother served in the United States Marine Corps and deployed to Viet Nam in 1968.

My first civilian assignment was as an internal auditor with the Department of the Navy in my home state. Very few military personnel were on base at that time because it was a new installation. Several years later, I transferred to an internal auditor position with the Department of the Army, where I interacted with and supervised military personnel. While serving as a civilian with the Department of Army, I developed working relationships with military dependents and spouses. I even became a surrogate aunt to many children of both officers and enlisted military personnel.

A former supervisor, Donald Fithian, whom I kept in contact with from my assignment with the United States Army Europe, called me and asked if I would come to Baghdad. He wanted me to assist him in establishing the Resource Management Office for the Coalition Provisional Authority (CPA) for Iraq. He told me that although there was danger, I would work in the well-protected "Green Zone area."

I told Don, "I will fast and pray for three days and seek guidance from the Holy Spirit." After three days of fasting and praying, I called Don. I told him to process the paperwork for my temporary duty orders.

Pentagon and Corp of Engineers personnel had two weeks of training and briefing before my departure. I remained in the nation's capital for two weeks. On the date of my scheduled departure to Kuwait, my mother had to be hospitalized in Georgia.

My mother's hospitalization presented me with an unforeseen dilemma. I had forgotten about the television coverage of the War in Viet Nam when I agreed to volunteer for a temporary duty assignment in Baghdad, Iraq during the Second Gulf War. Several months later, I understood from my youngest sister that mother stayed glued to the television reports of the war in Iraq.

Five months later, I received revelation through the Holy Spirit that I must be out of Iraq before the tenth of April that year. This was a dilemma because I had another month and a half left on my assignment.

Additionally, there were no commercial airline flights departing from Baghdad. What made it imperative for me to leave immediately was the fact that two contractors were beheaded the day before the resumption of commercial air flights.

Also, Iraqi rebels were killing Iraqi citizens who worked for the Coalition Provision Authority. Through the assistance of an Iraqi office worker, I successfully booked a flight on the first resumed commercial flight from Baghdad to Amman, Jordan. Talking about the Lord will make a way; yes, He did.

We often hear about the glory and honor of war, but we don't often talk about the other side of war. The side that's filled with pain, suffering, and loss. I've seen firsthand the devastation that war can cause. I've seen friends and fellow soldiers killed in battle. I've seen innocent civilians caught in the crossfire. I've seen families torn apart by loss. War is not glamorous or honorable. It is a tragedy. A tragedy that we should all do everything in our power to avoid. So, the next time you want to glorify war, remember the other side of war. Remember the pain, suffering, and loss that it causes. And let's all work together to build a better world.

Presidential Palace Chapel, Baghdad Iraq, where I
worshipped while deployed.

During her professional career, she lived and worked in Tanzania East Africa, Germany, and Iraq and in several states in U.S. Mary is a retired U.S. Department of Defense civil servant. She attended public and private school in Cordele, Ga.

Mary earned higher education degrees at Savannah State College (B.S in accounting), Syracuse University (MBA), and Georgia Southern University (MPA). She loves family, genealogy research, traveling, playing scrabble, reading, writing, and golf.

Mary was blessed to be the primary care giver for her centenarian mother. Mary is a business consultant. She assisted individuals with legal documents, research, taxes, and financial related matters. Mary is an independent business owner (business administration and health and wellness advocate).

Her literary works include *Luella Campbell Beal: A Force to Reckon With* is her first published literary work. Mary second published work is a sequel and is titled, *Help Me Cross Over from Earth to Heaven*. She is a contributing author in the recent released anthology, **Achieving Results**. She recently published, another non-fiction biographical about the life of a family friend, **How to Live Well Past 100 Years.** Mary volunteers as a Health and Wellness Advocate and is Blacks in Government Region IV health and wellness coordinator.

11

ENEMIES WITHIN THE RANKS
Takia Chase-Smith

I joined the military at the age of seventeen as a mechanic. My grandfather, mother, and cousin were all in the Army. I initially joined to make my mother proud. I wanted to be the next best thing in our family. I was a great Soldier when I was going through training. When I first reported. It was terrible. I ran my first mile in twenty-five minutes.

I had earned a physical fitness patch by the time I graduated from basic training. I was running two miles in 15:36. I could do seventy-eight sit-ups and forty-two pushups in two minutes. I loved working out at that point.

Moving on to my first job training. I loved it. However, that was my first taste of failure. I was one of two females in the class and had to compete with the other female. She beat me. Man, was that tough. When we graduated, she was named Soldier of the platoon, and I vowed to not be second again.

There is one training exercise in the Army when you low crawl the length of a football field with one arm on your weapon and the other to get you across. That was one of the scariest things of my life at that moment.

I had some of the best and worst times of my life all while in the military. When I returned home after training. I was pregnant. Without a book on how to parent, I had to grow up extremely fast, and I believe I have done quite well. In the military, there are regulations for everything. I wish babies were issued with one. (just kidding)

I gained several skills and trades before my second anniversary in the military and after the birth of my son. I became the best Admin Specialist I could be in my unit. I couldn't do my duties as a mechanic because of the pregnancy, so I learned everything I could about the new job. I also became a recruiter assistant.

Things got heavy. I was assaulted by someone that I respected. He was an outstanding Soldier and Senior NCO but a true scumbag and disgrace to the military. I was new to the organization and this put fear in me.

I didn't know whether to tell or just be quiet. I did report him; however, it was basically brushed under the rug. Even the EEO rep didn't take me seriously. I remember him saying well, you emailed him after your report, so did he really harm you? I was doing my job; that is why he was on the email.

My determination and dedication allowed me to be committed to the organization. This was a slap in the face. He stayed around but eventually, after being reported by so many, he was allowed to leave and go elsewhere. I'm sure without a doubt that he harmed many more Soldiers.

Shortly after, I was fired from my position because I took a leave of absence without permission. I went AWOL. I was so hurt and distraught that my coworkers and supervisors didn't believe in me, so after the situation, I took a small break.

After I returned, I wanted to continue to be dedicated to my Country and to my unit. I returned to work a few months later and gave it my all. I worked tirelessly and intended to be the best.

Since I was the best Admin in my unit when the unit was deployed, so was I. Although I wasn't on the original list and had no intention of going off, I went to the battlefield.

I was only nineteen years old, and I was in a WAR. Things overseas were much different than in America. I remember crying on the bus and not wanting to get off when we landed. Scared/afraid/terrified, none of those words could describe how I felt, but I strived and worked hard each day while over there. As the mortars came in and the bullets flew through the skies, enemies were behind the friendly fire lines.

After only a few months overseas, I was raped! This was a major setback for me. I was hurt, my motivation went down, and I was no longer eager to be number one.

I was betrayed. I didn't really care anymore about the uniform. I was in love with someone and didn't have the courage to tell him I had been raped. I didn't want to be embarrassed again. I didn't want this to make me lose my job.

I didn't want to be laughed at again, so I continued working as if nothing had happened. Later in life, it came back to haunt me. I will highly recommend that you tell and deal with the situation immediately after it happens. Because waiting only makes it worst.

This did not start or stop with me. After leaving the military in 2018 and speaking to other women, I learned that so many had been molested and raped while serving our Country. This is one of those things that only a few gather the nerve to speak on. As a victim and survivor, I encourage you to always speak your truth. Speak up for yourself even when you think others will not believe you.

I have spent years trying to forget these horrible events. Unfortunately, that will never happen, but I am healing within because I have chosen to speak on it. I can have free conversations today. Report it! I found the strength, and so will you.

Takia Chase-Smith is a Wife and Mother of three. She is a Veteran who specializes in helping youth with becoming authors and entrepreneurs while creating digital products.

Her hobbies include swimming, writing, reading, networking, and traveling. I have authored in several books to include Pendulum of a mother's love and Forgiveness: Making peace with your past.

"I started the Pendulum series so that I can close the gap between Mothers and Daughters."

I can be found on linktree as @TakiaChaseSmith Please follow my linktr.ee to keep up with my latest project.

ABOUT PA-PRO-VI PUBLISHING

The owner and founder of Pa-Pro-Vi is LaQuita Parks. Pa-Pro-Vi means pain, progress, victory because we believe that without pain there is no progress and without progress there can be no victory. We help people take their stories from a "thought to a realization!" We are located in the Riverdale, Georgia area. Contact us through our website at www.paprovipublishing.com

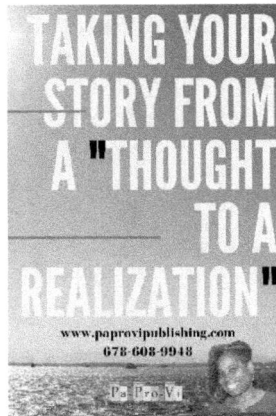

www.ingramcontent.com/pod-product-compliance
Lightning Source LLC
LaVergne TN
LVHW051234080426
835513LV00016B/1588